Number 116
Winter 2007

New Directions for E

D0513081

Process Use in Theory, Research, and Practice

J. Bradley Cousins
Editor

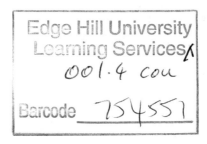
PROCESS USE IN THEORY, RESEARCH, AND PRACTICE
J. Bradley Cousins (ed.)
New Directions for Evaluation, no. 116
Sandra Mathison, Editor-in-Chief

Microfilm copies of issues and articles are available in 16mm and 35mm, as well as microfiche in 105mm, through University Microfilms Inc., 300 North Zeeb Road, Ann Arbor, Michigan 48106-1346.

New Directions for Evaluation is indexed in Cambridge Scientific Abstracts (CSA/CIG), Contents Pages in Education (T & F), Educational Research Abstracts Online (T & F), ERIC Database (Education Resources Information Center), Higher Education Abstracts (Claremont Graduate University), Social Services Abstracts (CSA/CIG), Sociological Abstracts (CSA/CIG), and Worldwide Political Sciences Abstracts (CSA/CIG).

NEW DIRECTIONS FOR EVALUATION (ISSN 1097-6736, electronic ISSN 1534-875X) is part of The Jossey-Bass Education Series and is published quarterly by Wiley Subscription Services, Inc., A Wiley Company, at Jossey-Bass, 989 Market Street, San Francisco, California 94103-1741.

SUBSCRIPTIONS cost $85 for U.S./Canada/Mexico; $109 international. For institutions, agencies, and libraries, $215 U.S.; $255 Canada/Mexico; $289 international. Prices subject to change.

EDITORIAL CORRESPONDENCE should be addressed to the Editor-in-Chief, Sandra Mathison, University of British Columbia, 2125 Main Mall, Vancouver, BC V6T 1Z4, Canada.

www.josseybass.com

Editorial Policy and Procedures

New Directions for Evaluation, a quarterly sourcebook, is an official publication of the American Evaluation Association. The journal publishes empirical, methodological, and theoretical works on all aspects of evaluation. A reflective approach to evaluation is an essential strand to be woven through every volume. The editors encourage volumes that have one of three foci: (1) craft volumes that present approaches, methods, or techniques that can be applied in evaluation practice, such as the use of templates, case studies, or survey research; (2) professional issue volumes that present issues of import for the field of evaluation, such as utilization of evaluation or locus of evaluation capacity; (3) societal issue volumes that draw out the implications of intellectual, social, or cultural developments for the field of evaluation, such as the women's movement, communitarianism, or multiculturalism. A wide range of substantive domains is appropriate for *New Directions for Evaluation;* however, the domains must be of interest to a large audience within the field of evaluation. We encourage a diversity of perspectives and experiences within each volume, as well as creative bridges between evaluation and other sectors of our collective lives.

The editors do not consider or publish unsolicited single manuscripts. Each issue of the journal is devoted to a single topic, with contributions solicited, organized, reviewed, and edited by a guest editor. Issues may take any of several forms, such as a series of related chapters, a debate, or a long article followed by brief critical commentaries. In all cases, the proposals must follow a specific format, which can be obtained from the editor-in-chief. These proposals are sent to members of the editorial board and to relevant substantive experts for peer review. The process may result in acceptance, a recommendation to revise and resubmit, or rejection. However, the editors are committed to working constructively with potential guest editors to help them develop acceptable proposals.

Sandra Mathison, Editor-in-Chief
University of British Columbia
2125 Main Mall
Vancouver, BC V6T 1Z4
CANADA
e-mail: nde@eval.org

CONTENTS

EDITOR'S NOTES

This volume arises from an American Evaluation Association (AEA) Presidential Strand session at Evaluation 2006 in Portland, Oregon, titled "Process Use—Towards a Fuller Definition of the Consequences of Evaluation." The panel was led by Michael Harnar, a graduate student at Claremont Graduate School, whose discomfort with the construct of "process use"—specifically its meaning and the inherent challenges of specifying it in operational terms—motivated him to organize the session. Thanks to Michael's initiative, participating panel members, among them Courtney Amo, Brad Cousins, Michael Harnar, Hallie Preskill, and Jean King, explored process use from methodological, empirical, and theoretical perspectives. Michael Patton, the originator of the term, ended the session with cross-cutting reflections. A perfect fit with the theme of Evaluation 2006—"Evaluation Consequences"—the session was timely because almost a decade had transpired since Patton coined the name for this unique form of evaluation impact. Panel sessions are not always successful, but this one fared quite well as defined by audience draw, interaction, and enthusiasm. But perhaps an even more telling indicator of the session's success is that it spawned this volume in which participating panel members have made contributions, joined by other colleagues—Fred Carden, Sarah Earl, Frances Lawrenz, Doug Huffman, Randy McGinnis, and Donna Podems—who graciously consented to move us beyond the elegant world of theory and research into the realities of evaluation practice by writing case narrative chapters.

Inquiry into the consequences of evaluation has evolved considerably over time, with the focus shifting from the problem of nonuse of evaluation to understanding conceptual, symbolic, and persuasive (as opposed to strictly instrumental) benefits, and to identifying a range of factors and conditions under which use would be more likely (Shulha and Cousins, 1997).

All of these conceptions of use were grounded within a common conception that use and influence could be traced to evaluation findings or to the knowledge outputs of evaluative activities. Yet a qualitatively different type of use and impact began to emerge from evaluation practice and research on it. This new sort of consequence—process use—appeared to be

Note: I would like to thank Sandra Mathison and anonymous members of the editorial advisory board for their input on my initial proposal for this volume. I would also like to acknowledge and thank the contributors, several of whom participated as peer reviewers for chapters in a single-blind process. Finally, thanks especially to Michael Harnar for showing considerable initiative in getting this ball rolling.

attributable to something wholly independent of evaluation findings—specifically, the activities or processes of evaluation, as opposed to its products or outputs.

Several years later, the term has been relatively well integrated into the parlance of evaluators and evaluation theorists. Process use has assisted in establishing empirical and conceptual links between evaluation use and organizational learning (for example, Cousins and Earl, 1995; Preskill and Torres, 1999; Shulha and Cousins, 1997); documenting consequences of participatory evaluation (Cousins, 2003; Cousins and Earl, 1995; King, 1995, 2002); demonstrating ties between evaluation use and cognate fields such as research use and knowledge use (for example, Cousins and Shulha, 2006); developing compelling arguments for moving beyond conceptions of use to understandings of evaluation influence, more broadly defined (Kirkhart, 2000; Henry and Mark, 2003; Mark and Henry, 2004); and understanding evaluation capacity building in emerging ways (for example, Compton, Glover-Kudon, Smith, and Avery, 2002; Cousins, Goh, Clark, and Lee, 2004).

Although the construct is relatively young, knowledge and understanding about process use have evolved to a sufficient level of maturity to warrant close systematic examination. This volume was compiled as a multifaceted exploration of process use that includes methodological, empirical, and conceptual inquiries, as well as rich narrative forays into the domain of evaluation practice. I believe such a comprehensive approach serves to deepen understanding of process use as pivotal in contemporary theory on evaluation consequences.

This volume begins with a review of empirical research by Amo and Cousins, whose main goal was to examine critically how theorists have conceptualized process use. Eighteen studies, many of them predating emergence of the term *process use*, were located and systematically analyzed. A number of these studies were indirect queries into process use, but some were direct, as is the case with the study reported by Harnar and Preskill in Chapter Two. They asked evaluators to reflect on what process use looks like. Written responses to an open-ended question from almost five hundred AEA-affiliated evaluators formed the data set for analysis. The rich findings are quite revealing in terms of variability in understanding and the meaning of process use espoused by the evaluators in the sample. Next, King endeavors to make sense of her practice over the years by reflecting on it using process use as a lens; in Chapter Three she produces a compelling list of considerations featuring process use in evaluation capacity building toward that enchanting (if not often sought after) place, "free range evaluation . . . evaluation thinking that lives unfettered in an organization."

Theory and research are essential, but they cannot be entirely meaningful in the absence of process use in practice. We are fortunate to have three contributions emerging from quite varying contexts, each with its own insights into practice. First, in Chapter Four, Carden and Earl walk us through the process of reforming a project-reporting process that is central to the evaluation function in a large Canadian international development research funding organization. Here, we witness powerful transforming effects of process use as the reporting process evolves from a mundane compliance-oriented chore to something far more meaningful to learning within the organization at numerous levels. Next, in Chapter Five, Lawrenz, Huffman, and McGinnis examine process use from the perspective of their National Science Foundation funded project—a large national, multilevel, multisite evaluation. Lawrenz and colleagues explore the challenges, dilemmas, and issues surrounding evaluation process use by stakeholders, including local-level evaluators. Finally, Podems introduces us to the stark reality of development evaluation in the context of South African HIV-AIDS intervention; Chapter Six is a richly detailed and compelling reflective narrative that might just be alternatively titled "accidental process use" or "making the best of things through evaluation capacity building."

This volume benefits from the same planned conclusion as did the Evaluation 2006 panel session on process use: words of wisdom from Patton. Chapter Seven is a combined reflection on process use and a synthesis or integration across the forerunning chapters in the volume. Among other interesting insights and commentary, Patton takes exception to the "quest for the holy grail" of seeking out standardized operationalizing of process use, favoring instead pursuit of what he sees as its real value as a "sensitizing construct." As has been mentioned, at the conclusion of Harnar's AEA panel session, there was a period of lively audience engagement and interaction with the panelists. On behalf of my colleagues, I can say that we hope for a similar conclusion here—that is, ongoing discussion, debate, and deliberation about process use in theory, research, and practice. This we would take as a marker of the volume's success.

References

Compton, D., Glover-Kudon, R., Smith, I. E., & Avery, M. E. Ongoing capacity building in the American Cancer Society (ACS) 1995–2001. In D. Compton, M. Baizerman, and S. H. Stockdill (eds.), *The Art, Craft and Science of Evaluation Capacity Building. New Directions for Evaluation*, no. 93. San Francisco: Jossey-Bass, 2002.

Cousins, J. B. "Utilization Effects of Participatory Evaluation." In T. Kellaghan, D. L. Stufflebeam, and L. A. Wingate (eds.), *International Handbook of Educational Evaluation*. Boston: Kluwer, 2003.

Cousins, J. B., and Earl, L. *Participatory Evaluation in Education: Studies in Evaluation Use and Organizational Learning*. London: Falmer, 1995.

Cousins, J. B., Goh, S., Clark, S., and Lee, L. "Integrating Evaluative Inquiry into the Organizational Culture: A Review and Synthesis of the Knowledge Base." *Canadian Journal of Program Evaluation*, 2004, *19*(2), 99–141.

Cousins, J. B., and Shulha, L. M. "A Comparative Analysis of Evaluation Utilization and Its Cognate Fields." In I. F. Staw, M. M. Mark, and J. Greene (eds.), *The Sage Handbook of Evaluation*, Thousand Oaks, Calif.: Sage, 2006.

Henry, G. T., and Mark, M. M. "Beyond Use: Understanding Evaluation's Influence on Attitudes and Actions." *American Journal of Evaluation*, 2003, *24*, 293–314.

King, J. A. "Involving Practitioners in Evaluation Studies: How Viable Is Collaborative Evaluation in Schools?" In J. B. Cousins and L. M. Earl (eds.), *Participatory Evaluation in Education: Studies in Evaluation Use and Organizational Learning.* London: Falmer, 1995.

King, J. A. "Building the Evaluation Capacity of a School District." In D. Compton, M. Baizerman, and S. H. Stockdill (eds.), *The Art, Craft and Science of Evaluation Capacity Building. New Directions for Evaluation*, no. 93. San Francisco: Jossey-Bass, 2002.

Kirkhart, K. "Reconceptualizing Evaluation Use: An Integrated Theory of Influence." In V. Carcelli and H. Preskill (eds.), *The Expanding Scope of Evaluation Use. New Directions for Evaluation*, no. 88. San Francisco: Jossey-Bass, 2000.

Mark, M. M., and Henry, G. T. "The Mechanisms and Outcomes of Evaluation Influence." *Evaluation*, 2004, *10*, 35–57.

Preskill, H., and Torres, R. T. *Evaluative Inquiry for Learning in Organizations.* Thousand Oaks, Calif.: Sage, 1999.

Shulha, L. M., and Cousins J. B. "Evaluation Use: Theory, Research and Practice Since 1986." *Evaluation Practice*, 1997, *18*, 195–208.

J. Bradley Cousins
Editor

J. BRADLEY COUSINS is a professor of educational administration in the Faculty of Education, University of Ottawa, and editor-in-chief of the Canadian Journal of Program Evaluation.

NEW DIRECTIONS FOR EVALUATION • DOI: 10.1002/ev

1

The authors draw on empirical research on evaluation to consider how process use has been operationalized to date and what this may mean for ongoing research in this area.

Going Through the Process: An Examination of the Operationalization of Process Use in Empirical Research on Evaluation

Courtney Amo, J. Bradley Cousins

The study of the consequences of evaluation, or more specifically of evaluation use or utilization,[1] represents a significant portion of the body of research on evaluation (Alkin, 2003). Much has been written on the evolution of the multidimensional concept of evaluation use, most recently the examination of consequences of evaluation that are not a function of evaluation findings or recommendations, but rather of the *process* of evaluation in its own right (Alkin and Taut, 2003; Cousins, Goh, Clark, and Lee, 2004; Preskill, Zuckerman, and Matthews, 2003). Although Patton (1997) was the first to define *process use* as the impacts that result from the learning occurring as a consequence of involvement in the evaluation process, other researchers have noted earlier evidence of this type of evaluation "use" (Cousins and Earl, 1992; Cousins and Leithwood, 1993; King and Pechman, 1984; Greene, 1988). In addition, the effects of involvement in applied, systematic inquiry have been mentioned in the literature on participatory action research (Whyte, 1990), knowledge use (Dunn and Holtzner, 1988), and other forms of collaborative inquiry (Levin, 1993).

Note: We would like to thank Michael Harnar for proposing the American Evaluation Association panel session for which an earlier version of this chapter was prepared. The invitation to participate in this session encouraged us to take an in-depth look at this important evaluation consequence.

Conceptual and theoretical work on process use (for example, Alkin and Taut, 2003; Fetterman, 2003; Patton, 1997) has begun to spark empirical research (for example, Morabito, 2002; Preskill and Caracelli, 1997; Preskill, Zuckerman, and Matthews, 2003; Taut, 2005; Turnbull, 1998, 1999) that is increasing understanding and use of the concept in informing evaluation practice (Patton, 1998). Our interest in this chapter is twofold: (1) to consider how the construct of process use has been operationalized in empirical research examining process use directly or indirectly and (2) to describe the types of research that have been carried out, with an eye to developing an agenda for ongoing research in this area.

As is discussed here, Patton's definition of process use (1997) has influenced the design of the majority of the empirical research reviewed in this chapter:

> Process use refers to and is indicated by individual changes in thinking and behavior, and program or organizational changes in procedures and culture, that occur among those involved in evaluation as a result of the learning that occurs during the evaluation process. Evidence of process use is represented by statements such as this one after an evaluation: 'The impact on our program came not just from the findings but also from going through the thinking process that the evaluation required'. [Patton, 1997, p. 90]

This by-product of evaluation is consistent with constructivist-learning theory, which purports that learning is a social process (Bandura, 1986) and that groups of people make meaning through the process of conducting an evaluation (Preskill, 2005). Process use has thus been linked to collaborative, participatory, empowerment, utilization-focused, and learning-oriented approaches to evaluation that advocate various levels of direct or indirect involvement of stakeholders in the evaluation process (Cousins and Earl, 1992; Fetterman, 1997, 2003; Preskill and Caracelli, 1997; Preskill, Zuckerman, and Matthews, 2003).

Process use also presents itself as the conceptual cousin of other observed consequences of evaluation, such as organizational learning (Cousins, Goh, Clark, and Lee, 2004; Preskill, 1994), evaluation capacity building (Stockdill, Baizerman, and Compton, 2002), and evaluation influence (Kirkhart, 2000). The conceptual framework presented in Figure 1.1, which emerged from a recent study by Cousins, Goh, Clark, and Lee (2004) on the conceptual interconnections and linkages among evaluation utilization, evaluation capacity building, and organizational learning, helps to situate process use in a larger context. Evaluative inquiry is conceived as an organizational support structure that leads to particular organizational consequences, namely evaluation consequences manifested as knowledge production, use of findings, and process use. Process use, in turn, is thought to enhance organizational readiness for evaluation through augmenting organizational capacity to do and use evaluation.

Although process use is present in conceptual literature on evaluation use, it has thus far seldom been put to empirical test. As evaluation theorists

Figure 1.1. Conceptual Framework of Evaluative Inquiry as an Organizational Learning System

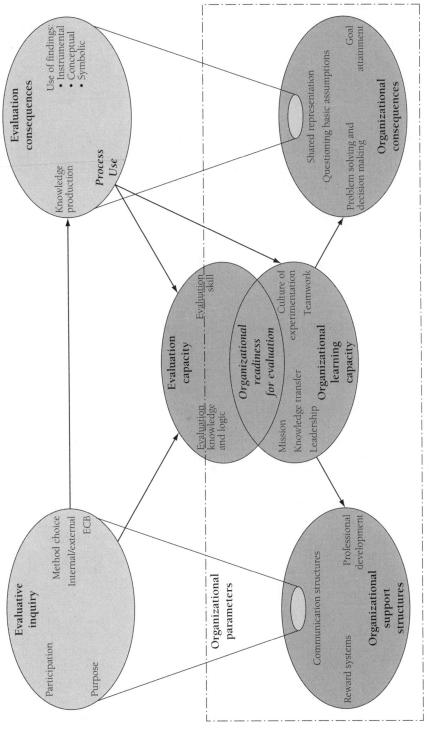

Source: Adapted from Cousins, Goh, Clark, and Lee (2004).

call for more research on the influence of evaluation on individual-level cognitive processes and interpersonal behaviors (for example, Henry and Mark, 2003) and as process use moves from being seen as a positive, incidental consequence of evaluation toward a goal evaluators aim to achieve through their approaches and methods (personal communication, M. Harnar, Mar. 2006), the need to provide empirical support for the concept becomes more pressing.

We now turn to a description of the methods used to identify empirical research concerned with process use and then to a description of the sample of studies we located. What follows is an analysis of these studies in terms of their operationalization of process use. We conclude with some thoughts on an agenda for ongoing research.

Method and Sample Characteristics

Direct and indirect empirical studies of process use were identified through a search of all relevant databases using the CSA Illumina Search Platform[2] and Proquest's Digital Dissertations. The following search terms were used: "evaluation utilization," "evaluation use," "organizational learning," "evaluation capacity," "knowledge utilization," "process use," and "process outcome." Bibliographic follow-up was used to complete the initial sample. Studies based on systematic observation of process use, including reflective accounts based on one or more case examples, were identified. We chose to include reflective accounts as they are based on observations made by evaluators or others and because they offer a rich source of information about complex phenomena in practical contexts. We retained eighteen studies for analysis.

Each study was content-analyzed to establish its operationalization of process use, which, for the purpose of this study, is defined as the process of translating an abstract construct into concrete measures for the purpose of observing the construct (Bouchard and Cyr, 1998; Greenstein, 2006). Although there are no steadfast rules for judging the appropriateness of an operationalization, *construct validity*—which refers to the degree of association between a theoretical construct or concept and its operationalization (Bouchard and Cyr, 1998; Greenstein, 2006)—constitutes a framework for gathering evidence in support of a particular operationalization. In this context, an operationalization showing evidence of construct validity would include (1) definition of the object of study grounded in the literature; (2) definition of the underlying concepts that make up the object of study (if applicable); (3) definitions of related constructs and concepts in order to differentiate the object of study; and (4) indicators and measures in order to assess the occurrence, quantity, or quality of the object of study (Cohen, Manion, and Morrison, 2000; Fraenkel and Wallen, 2003; Trochim, 2006).

A one-page summary was prepared for each study, outlining its context; purpose and research questions; design, methods, sampling, and unit of analysis; direct or indirect study of process use; operationalization of process use (including conceptual source); and relevant findings. These one-page summaries represent the first distillation of the raw data for this study.

Table 1.1 presents the descriptive characteristics of the sample of empirical studies selected for analysis. The studies are ordered by year of publication, and they appeared in the period 1984–2005. As a measure of quality control, we restricted our search to only peer-reviewed sources. All but three of the studies presented were published in peer-reviewed journals; Kamm (2004) and Taut (2005) are Ph.D. dissertations, and Cousins (1995) appeared in a volume coedited by the author. The sample of studies reflects a strong orientation toward qualitative research, primarily involving case studies (that is, longitudinal, exploratory, reflective, or descriptive). Also present are quantitative field studies yielding a mix of closed-form questionnaire data with written comments (for example, Cousins, Donohue, and Bloom, 1996; Preskill and Caracelli, 1997; Turnbull, 1998). In more than half of the studies (eleven of eighteen), and particularly in those appearing before 2000, examination of process use (or of earlier conceptions) was not the primary focus of the study. Direct investigations of process use followed Patton's inclusion of the construct as a chapter in his third revision of *Utilization-Focused Evaluation* (1997).

Operationalization of Process Use

The basic requirements for operationalization outlined earlier were applied to the sample of studies selected for this analysis. Table 1.2 presents the results of this examination.

Defining Process Use. All but four of the studies (for example, Brett, Hill-Mead, and Wu, 2000) presented an *explicit* definition of process use or of the similar concept being examined as it relates to their study, and all but four again (for example, Preskill, Zuckerman, and Matthews, 2003) gave definitions of other utilization constructs related to process use, which help to differentiate and delineate process use. Although a few of the studies examined process use as it *emerged* in the research (as with Cousins, 1995) and a few others drew the concept from an implicit understanding of the literature (Turnbull, 1998), the majority have proposed definitions of process use (or similar concepts) grounded in the body of literature on evaluation use and on collaborative inquiry in evaluation (see, for example, Greene, 1988; Kirkhart, 2000; Patton, 1997).

Here is a brief overview of some of the key definitional shifts that have shaped the study of process use.

One of the first studies found to mention a concept similar to process use is that of King and Pechman (1984). Emergent from this case study, which aimed at broadening and validating conceptualizations of evaluation use that were present at the time (instrumental, persuasive, and conceptual use of findings), is the concept of "charged use," or use that "carries with it the potential for disruption or change" (p. 244). Although the authors mention in

Table 1.1. Descriptive Characteristics of Empirical Studies (in Chronological Order)

Study	Sample	Context	Design and Methods	Purpose, Research Questions	Direct or Indirect Study of Process Use	Operationalization of Process Use
King and Pechman (1984)	Research and evaluation unit in large-city central office; USA	Evaluation use in school systems	Longitudinal (one-year) case study; naturalistic observation (interviews, field notes)	Discuss evolving evaluation use literature; process of local evaluation use; categories of evaluation use; implications of case study results	Indirect	"Charged use": use with potential for disruption or change; triggered by interactions between potential user and informal evaluation information (including conversation)
Cousins and Leithwood (1993)	Two hundred thirty-three elementary school principals and one hundred fifty-five central board office staff members; Canada	Examination of initiatives designed to support school improvement as a result of a provincial review of educational practice	Exploratory field surveys	Examine the contribution of a relatively comprehensive set of variables influencing knowledge use; test power of knowledge utilization framework in explaining observed use	Indirect	"Interactive processes": interaction or linkages between researchers and practitioners; involvement of practitioners in the research process (social processing, engagement, involvement, and ongoing contact)
Forss, Cracknell, and Samset (1994)	Eleven background reports; eight case studies; survey and interviews of staff (n unclear); international	Improving effectiveness of Norwegian development assistance	Meta-evaluation; case study of eight evaluations; questionnaires, interviews, document review	Explore role, impact, contribution of evaluation in organizational learning; explore ways of increasing evaluation contribution to organizational learning	Indirect	"Learning by involvement": characterized by program officer taking part in evaluations and project reviews and developing knowledge and external expertise

Cousins (1995)	Two case school districts; Canada	School district use of evaluative inquiry to support school improvement	Comparative case study design: high vs. marginal success; interview, document analysis	Examine extent to which evaluation was used and factors fostering or inhibiting use	Indirect	Development of research skills, educator professional development function of participating in evaluation study
Cousins, Donohue, and Bloom (1996)	Members of professional evaluation and education associations: AEA (n = 306), CES (n = 200), AERA (n = 35), AERO (n = 23); Canada, USA	Assessing perceptions of evaluators and evaluation scholars regarding collaborative evaluation	Exploratory research study; survey	Examine perceptions regarding collaborative evaluation; establish extent to which practitioners find collaborative or participatory approaches useful; portray various collaborative practices and processes	Indirect	Survey questionnaire items address impact of stakeholder participation in evaluation (participation helps bring about social justice; develops research skills; learning about evaluation as change strategy)
Preskill and Caracelli (1997)	Members of AEA Evaluation Use TIG (n = 282); USA	Assessing evaluators' perceptions about evaluation use	Exploratory research study; survey	Explore linkages between theories of evaluation use and perspectives of practice; obtain past and current perceptions and experiences with evaluation use	Direct	"Refers to the cognitive and behavioral changes resulting from users' engagement in the evaluation process. Process use occurs when those involved in the evaluation learn from the evaluation process itself." (p. 217)

(Continued)

Table 1.1. Continued

Study	Sample	Context	Design and Methods	Purpose, Research Questions	Direct or Indirect Study of Process Use	Operationalization of Process Use
Lau and LeMahieu (1997)	n/a; USA	Evaluation of Humanities Education, Research, and Language Development (HERALD) project, California School District	Reflective case study; written from perspective of evaluators	Discuss theoretical underpinnings and execution of evaluation design aimed at empowering teachers	Indirect	Effects of teacher-evaluator collaboration, effects of participation in evaluation process (teachers as internal evaluators)
Turnbull (1998)	Three hundred eight elementary and secondary school teachers; Canada	British Columbia School Accreditation Program	Exploratory and confirmatory case study; questionnaire	To develop and test second-order confirmatory factor analytic model of conceptual, instrumental, and symbolic use	Indirect	Survey questionnaire items on conceptual use show overlap with process use (process gave better understanding of strengths and weaknesses of school; activities provided necessary knowledge to contribute to development of school growth plan)
Turnbull (1999)	Three hundred fifteen elementary and secondary school teachers; Canada	British Columbia School Accreditation Program	Exploratory (or confirmatory?) case study; questionnaire	To gain better understanding of participatory evaluation by testing causal relations in proposed model of participatory evaluation	Indirect	"Participatory efficacy": "refers to the degree to which expected or assumed outcomes of participatory evaluation have been achieved" (p. 133); survey questionnaire items relate to process use (learned useful things about school;

					activities provided necessary knowledge to contribute to development of school growth plan; better understanding of points of view of other staff)
Brett, Hill-Mead, and Wu (2000)	n/a; USA	Evaluation use in national not-for-profit youth services organization (City Year) with centralized evaluation department	Reflective case study; written from perspective of evaluator and two staff members	Discuss how organization's relationship with evaluation evolved; how evaluation has been used; lessons learned on enhancing evaluation use and influence	Indirect	Provides examples of impact of involvement in evaluation process (enhanced understanding of evaluation function; better appreciation of outcome orientation; forum for forced reflection; sense of ownership; ability to mentor others; strengthened services; organizational change)
Shulha (2000)	n/a; Colombia	Influence of participatory, evaluative inquiry process in assessing need for university-school learning partnership between large Canadian university and large pre-K through 12 international school in Colombia	Reflective case study, written from point of view of evaluator	Show evaluative inquiry as potent alternative to classic forms of professional development; demonstrate challenges and results of rooting university-school learning partnership in evaluative inquiry; analyze utility of process using Kirkhart's theory of integrated influence (2000)	Indirect	Shows impact of involvement in evaluative inquiry through lens of theory of integrated influence; impact evidenced by observation (including discussions of learning (e.g., skills development), actions (decision making), affective changes (independence), and other effects (de facto public declaration of commitment)

(Continued)

Table 1.1. Continued

Study	Sample	Context	Design and Methods	Purpose, Research Questions	Direct or Indirect Study of Process Use	Operationalization of Process Use
Russ-Eft, Atwood, and Egherman (2002)	Twenty-three salespeople, ten implementation specialists, nine consultants, forty representatives of client companies; USA	Evaluation of a sales program within a business services organization (XYZ Corporation) in the USA	Descriptive case study; interviews, surveys	Explore use and nonuse of evaluation results, with particular emphasis on process use; factors contributing to use and nonuse of private sector evaluation	Direct	Patton (1997) definition; process use indicated by enhanced shared understanding, supported and reinforced program intervention, increased engagement, self-determination, ownership
Morabito (2002)	n/a; USA	A U.S. school that provides instruction to physically and medically disabled children K–12	Reflective case study; written from perspective of evaluator	What specific evaluator roles, philosophies, and interpersonal dynamics hold the potential to foster process influence	Direct	"Process influence": capacity of evaluation process to affect organizational stakeholders and entity being evaluated, as evidenced (in this case) by individual and team learning, changes in school structure and curriculum
Forss, Rebien, and Carlsson (2002)	Not specified; international	Evaluation of Nordic Development Fund (NDF, small enterprise development program) and of effectiveness of expatiate experts on aid programs	Meta-evaluation; review of literature, interviews, two case studies	Explore process uses of evaluation, develop typology of process use, generate hypotheses regarding context and activities relating to process use of evaluations	Direct	Defined as "utility to stakeholders of being involved in the planning and implementation of an evaluation" (p. 30), and evidenced by learning to learn, developing professional networks, creating shared understanding, strengthening project, boosting morale

	Sample	Program evaluated	Methods	Purpose	Type	Definition
Preskill, Zuckerman, and Matthews (2003)	Sixteen interviews with advisory group members and senior administrators of American Cancer Society; USA	Yearly evaluation of the Tell a Friend program and ACS in USA	Exploratory case study of two evaluations; interviews	Explore what and how advisory group members learned from involvement in evaluation process; add to list of process use variables (Preskill, 2000) factors that support or hinder learning	Direct	"We view process use as the learning that occurs from being involved in any phase of the evaluation process" (p. 427), as evidenced by learning about evaluation, learning about the program, and gaining overall evaluation experience
Kamm (2004)	Seventeen staff members (eight inquiry team members, nine nonmembers); USA	Examination of the effects of implementing the EILO (Evaluative Inquiry for Learning in Organizations) approach with the administration, staff, and clients of a small women's health education organization within a U.S. hospital	Longitudinal case study (during and postintervention); individual and focus group interviews, observations, document and artifact review, survey	Learn about effects of implementing EILO approach within health education organization; study of effects on organization and on people involved, and issues surrounding implementation process	Direct	Process use occurs when "individual changes in thinking and behavior, and program or organizational changes in procedures and culture ... occur among those involved in evaluation as a result of the learning that occurs during the evaluation process" (Patton, 1997, p. 90; p. 180); process use evidenced by individual and organizational learning, changes in individual and organizational behaviors, and affective changes in individuals

(Continued)

Table 1.1. Continued

Study	Sample	Context	Design and Methods	Purpose, Research Questions	Direct or Indirect Study of Process Use	Operationalization of Process Use
Sutherland (2004)	Forty-six teachers, administrators, students, parents at Edison Project school plus twelve district administrators; USA	Use of evaluation as part of commitment to be an Edison Project school, major funded school reform initiative	Longitudinal case study; observation and interview	How do the processes of data use and management feed into culture of continuous improvement?	Indirect	Data use integrated into the organization over time; extrinsic motivators become less important and intrinsic motivators are elevated as evaluation is integrated into organizational culture
Taut (2005)	Survey sample (n = 215 directors, professionals, and support staff; interview sample not specified; Europe	Study of the effectiveness of custom-made, self-evaluation capacity building interventions to foster learning from evaluation at a large international development cooperation organization	Action research, involving embedded case study, survey, document analysis, personal interview, participant observation, group discussion, informal communication	Address how evaluation in UNESCO can more effectively fulfill its learning purpose; how self-evaluation contributes to learning, prerequisites, constraints, and supporting factors for learning, intended and unintended outcomes of interventions in terms of process use, explanations of effectiveness and sustainability	Direct	Provides conceptual framework linking evaluation capacity building (elements of intervention), indicators of changes as a result of intervention (knowledge about evaluation, attitude toward evaluation, perceived ownership of process, skills to conduct evaluation tasks, and motivation to engage), and final outcomes of the intervention in terms of use of evaluation for learning (increased conceptual use of external evaluation processes and findings, increased integration of self-evaluative thinking and inquiry into work habits)

passing a possible link between changes in individuals' *attitude* over time as a product or impact of the evaluation process, they more clearly demonstrate changes in *actions* or *behaviors* as an effect of the interaction between nonevaluator stakeholders and the evaluation process through the examples given as evidence: "When an evaluator merely asked the director of a federal project why certain assistant teachers had attended an in-service workshop, the director realized that their attendance was inappropriate, and they were not included in the next session" (King and Pechman, 1984, p. 246).

Further early evidence of the effects of involving stakeholders in the evaluation process is found in a study by Cousins and Leithwood (1993) on the relative influence of knowledge utilization variables on educators' use of information for improvement purposes. "Interactive processes," a construct that emerged from Cousins' doctoral dissertation (1988) on school principals' use of data on their own performance, refers to the "processes that lie between disseminators of information and [the information's] actual use in practice-based communities . . ." (Cousins and Leithwood, 1993, pp. 310–311). Four categories of such processes (social processing, engagement, involvement, and ongoing contact) resulted in a number of learning, behavioral, and affective changes (such as personal and professional growth, organized reflection, and modification of practice) in individuals involved in local in-service activities. Although, in both these cases, it could be argued that changes resulting from interaction with information is evidence of use of findings rather than use of process, since the process of conducting an evaluation inherently involves extensive interactions with information, we would argue that the line cannot be drawn so clearly.

In their study of the link between evaluation and organizational learning in the context of a Norwegian development assistance organization, Forss, Cracknell, and Samset (1994) found that evaluations result in *learning* in two ways: through involvement in the evaluation process and through receipt of evaluation information via communication. Although learning through communication of evaluation information is seen as having more of an organizational-level impact, learning by involvement "may lead to rapid development of knowledge structures at the level of individuals and sections within the organization" (p. 585).

In response to a need to bridge the gap between theoretical interest in collaborative approaches to evaluation and their actual and perceived practical use and usefulness, Cousins, Donohue, and Bloom (1996) surveyed a sample of evaluators and evaluation scholars on their perceptions and practices regarding collaborative evaluation. The potential effects of stakeholder participation were explored through questionnaire items that spoke to the learning and behavioral impacts that are characteristic of process use; for example, "practitioners' participation in evaluation helps to bring about social justice" (p. 216) and "intended users have developed (or will develop) their research skills" (p. 220).

The following year, Patton (1997) formally defined process use as "individual changes in thinking and behavior, and program or organizational

Table 1.2. Process Use Operationalization in Empirical Studies

Study	Operationalization of Process Use				Unit of Analysis	Type of Process Use			
	Process Use Defined	Related Concepts Defined	Indicators and Measures Defined	Conceptual Source		Learning	Action or Behavior	Attitude and Affect	Other
King and Pechman (1984)	Similar concept: charged use	Yes	Researcher observation	Emergent	Individual		✓	✓	
Cousins and Leithwood (1993)	Similar concept: interactive processes, social processing	Yes	Perceptions of respondents (written)	Preordinate (Cousins, 1988; Greene, 1988; Huberman, 1987, 1990; Louis and Dentler, 1988)	Individual	✓	✓	✓	
Forss, Cracknell, and Samset (1994)	Similar concept defined	Yes	Evidence in documents, perceptions of respondents	Emergent	Individual and group	✓			
Cousins (1995)	Similar concept: research skills; professional development	Yes	Evidence in interviews with nonevaluator participants	Emergent	Individual	✓		✓	
Cousins, Donohue, and Bloom (1996)	Similar concept: benefits of collaborative inquiry	N/a	Evaluators' recall of effects of collaborative evaluation (ratings)	Preordinate (Cousins and Leithwood, 1993; Cousins and Earl, 1992, 1995)	Individual	✓	✓		✓
Preskill and Caracelli (1997)	Yes	Yes	Perceptions of respondents (ratings)	Preordinate (Greene, 1988; Patton, 1997)	Individual, group, organizational	✓	✓	✓	
Lau and LeMahieu (1997)	No, implicit in text	No	Evaluator observations	N/a (although idea to implement collaborative approach is grounded in the literature)	Group	✓	✓	✓	
Turnbull (1998)	No, implicit in text	Yes	Perceptions of respondents (ratings)	N/a (although conceptions of use are grounded in the literature)	Individual	✓	✓		
Turnbull (1999)	Similar concept defined	Yes	Perceptions of respondents (ratings)	Preordinate (Brunner and Guzman, 1989; Cousins and Earl, 1992; Garaway, 1995; Green and Southard, 1995; Newman and Cai, 1995; Patton, 1997; Weiss, 1983)	Individual	✓	✓	✓	

Study					Level			
Brett, Hill-Mead, and Wu (2000)	No, implicit in text	Yes	Participant observation	Preordinate (Patton, 1997, but not explicitly stated)	Organizational (site and national levels)	✓	✓	✓
Shulha (2000)	No, implicit in text	No	Participant observation	Preordinate (concept drawn from a number of fields of inquiry: collaborative research, cognitive development and structures of learning, student assessment, learning in organizations, knowledge utilization; example references provided)	Individual and organizational	✓	✓	✓
Russ-Eft, Atwood, and Egherman (2002)	Yes	Yes	Perceptions of respondents, participant observations	Preordinate (Patton, 1997)	Individual and organizational	✓	✓	
Morabito (2002)	Yes (but called process influence)	No	Participant observation	Preordinate (Patton, 1997; Kirkhart, 2000)	Group and organizational	✓	✓	
Forss, Rebien, and Carlsson (2002)	Yes	Yes	Participant observation, perceptions of interviewees	Preordinate (Patton, 1997, 1998)	Individual	✓	✓	✓
Preskill, Zuckerman, and Matthews (2003)	Yes	No	Perceptions of respondents (interviews)	Preordinate (Patton, 1997; Preskill, 2000)	Individual	✓	✓	
Kamm (2004)	Yes	Yes	Participant observation, perceptions of participants	Preordinate (Patton, 1997); also draws from Patton (1994), Fetterman (1996), Mertens and others (1994)	Individual and organizational	✓	✓	
Sutherland (2004)	Yes	Yes	Interviews with educator participants	Preordinate (Patton, 1997, 1998; Preskill, 2003)	Organizational	✓	✓	
Taut (2005)	Yes	Yes	Researcher observation, participant self-report (ratings)	Preordinate (Patton, 1997; but also Cousins, 2003; Forss, Rebien, and Carlsson, 2002; Alkin and Taut, 2003)	Individual, group, organizational	✓	✓	

changes in procedures and culture, that occur among those involved in the evaluation as a result of the learning that occurs during the evaluation process" (p. 90). Preskill and Caracelli (1997) used an adapted version of this definition in a survey examining, among other things, the perceptions of evaluators as to the distinction between process use and the use of findings. Although Patton's definition of process use speaks to changes in thinking and behavior, results of this survey point to changes in attitude or *affect* brought up earlier by King and Pechman (1984) and Greene (1988). Preskill and Caracelli report that "nearly two-thirds of survey respondents agree that evaluation can lead to empowerment or self-determination of individuals through internalizing evaluation processes" (p. 218).

Although the term *process use* had by then emerged in the conceptual and theoretical literature, it would take a few more years before it found its way, in a direct sense, into the empirical studies sampled for review. For instance, Turnbull (1998, 1999) examines the effects of participatory evaluation on teachers involved in a school accreditation program but does not specifically refer to process use. It is also interesting to note that other studies mention process use (Brett, Hill-Mead, and Wu, 2000; Shulha, 2000) but do not explicitly define the term as it related to their study. Morabito (2002) draws on Patton's definition (1997) but calls the concept "process influence," as a result of Kirkhart's reconceptualization of evaluation use as evaluation *influence* (2000). Subsequent studies (Russ-Eft, Atwood, and Egherman, 2002; Preskill, Zuckerman, and Matthews, 2003; Kamm, 2004; Taut, 2005) make explicit use of Patton's definition of process use (1997).

Forss, Rebien, and Carlsson (2002) draw from Patton's identification of four primary kinds of process use (enhancing shared understandings; supporting and reinforcing the program through intervention-oriented evaluation; increasing participants' engagement, sense of ownership, and self-determination; and program or organizational development) and from additional types of process use that Patton (1998) suggested (learning to learn, qualitative insights, and goal displacement) in defining process use. Forss and colleagues expand on the concept of process use by suggesting that developing professional networks and boosting morale—categories that emerged from their case studies—were evidence of process use.

Although Patton's definition of process use mentions involvement in the evaluation process as a necessary element of process use, the link between process use and the level or intensity of involvement of stakeholders in the evaluation process was not explored explicitly in the studies reviewed.

Measuring Process Use. Table 1.2 shows little variability in the indicators and measures of process use. Observation of process use and self-reported perceptions regarding process use serve well to document the *occurrence* of process use but less well to assess other qualifiers and quantifiers of the phenomenon (such as type, depth, range, amount) or of its nonoccurrence.

In contrast to the lack of variability in indicators or measures of process use, the sample of studies chosen for review shows variability in the unit of analysis, that is, studying process use at the individual (fourteen studies), group (five), or organization level (eight). Although Patton's definition (1997) accommodates process use at all three levels, case study approaches invariably focus the lens through which process use is examined.

Three broad *types* of process use, or what was considered evidence of process use, emerged from this review: process use as evidenced by *learning* (seventeen cases), by changes in *actions* or *behaviors* (fifteen), by changes in *affect* or *attitude* (thirteen), and by a few other impacts that do not fit neatly into these categories (social justice, opportunity, networking, and so on). Table 1.3 presents a preliminary grouping of evidence of process use presented across studies. Although this grouping is preliminary and reflects a certain amount of overlap across categories, it highlights the variety of impacts that have been observed as evidence of the benefits of going through the evaluation process.

Here are specific examples of process use summarized in Table 1.3 in more detail:

> Through being involved directly in the evaluation process and working closely with external evaluators, teachers no longer feared experimenting with new ways and being held accountable to outcomes. They had input into what was authentic in evaluating the new instructional practices, and evaluation became a non-threatening objective to inform change [Lau and LeMahieu, 1997, p. 13].

> City Year has come to appreciate other uses for evaluation. It has recognized that evaluation is a key capacity for an organization that wants to be both a learning organization and one that is "built to last" [Brett, Hill-Mead, and Wu, 2000, p. 83].

> The results of this study indicate significant process use throughout the inquiry. The majority of participants reported learning from the evaluation process itself. Four compelling examples of process use that occurred during this study are discussed here: (1) learning about the Parenting Education Initiative, (2) learning about evaluation in general and [about Evaluative Inquiry for Learning in Organizations (EILO)] in particular, (3) recognizing [and acting on] other opportunities for learning, and (4) [learning and using] the four EILO learning processes [Kamm, 2004, p. 184].

Implications and Conclusions

The literature search conducted in the context of this study, although not exhaustive, shows a relative paucity of empirical studies examining the concept of process use directly or indirectly. Almost a decade after the concept was coined, there remains much opportunity to study, question, and substantiate process use. Within the group of more recent studies reviewed,

Table 1.3. What Counts as Process Use?

Learning	Action or Behavior	Attitude and Affect	Other
• Enlightenment • Concept development • Confirming prior impressions • Awareness of key issues • Knowledge development (about evaluation in general, evaluative inquiry, benefits of evaluation) • Expertise development • Research skills, ability to implement elements of evaluation inquiry • Cognitive changes • Greater shared understanding • Ability to train others • Learning to learn, ability to recognize other learning opportunities • Learning about program, intervention, organization	• Not repeating previous action • Deciding to act on feedback from evaluator, on basis of participation in process • Requesting assistance from evaluator • Modifying practice, integrating evaluative inquiry in work practices • Using evaluation data, results, findings • Using evaluation skills • Changing behavior • Developing plan • Developing indicators, recommendations • Transferring decision-making power • Acting on other opportunities for learning	• Improved morale • Personal growth • Professional growth • Self-examination • Empowerment, belief in ability to influence change • Self-determination • Better understanding, respect of others • Appreciation of evaluation • Sense of ownership • Fostered independence • Role reconceptualization • Enhanced political self-esteem • Increased engagement • Desire to keep using skills	• Shared experience • Organized reflection • Social justice • Program and project changes, strengthening of service • Organizational improvement, development • Creation of relationships, developing professional networks • Opportunity (to test out partnerships) • Public declaration of commitment (by being part of evaluation group) • Overall evaluation experience

Patton's conceptualization of process use (1997) has been a solid backbone for research in this area. In addition, other ways of thinking about process use (for example, process influence rather than use; Kirkhart, 2000) have emerged. However, it would be fair to conclude at this point that empirical research on process use is in its infancy, and more and different research will be required to move this area of inquiry forward.

In their recent review and synthesis of the knowledge base linking evaluation utilization, evaluation capacity building, and organizational learning, Cousins, Goh, Clark, and Lee (2004) point to important methodological challenges that are also quite relevant to the ongoing study of process use. Although reflective case studies are important and necessary, they are limited in that they tend not to present multiple interpretations of events. Such studies are essential to developing an understanding of process use, but the field would also benefit from more deeply systematic approaches to inquiry that show greater variability in design and methods, and stronger methodological sophistication.

In addition, this review shows little variability in how process use has been measured, but high variability in what has been included as evidence of process use. Although conceptual and theoretical work (for example, Alkin and Taut, 2003; Patton, 1997) has offered a solid basis for a process use conceptual framework to emerge, there is also a need to empirically test and confirm ideas and assumptions presented thus far. For instance, to what extent or depth do nonevaluator stakeholders need to be involved in the evaluation process in order to experience process use? In sum, empirical studies of process use have yet to show strong evidence of construct validity through operationalization of process use.

This study presents a picture of the state of empirical research on process use thus far and should help to encourage building a balanced and strong knowledge base on process use that can help inform future debates on the theoretical, empirical, and practical implications of this important consequence of evaluation.

Notes

1. Evaluation use and evaluation utilization are considered synonyms in this chapter, as is the case in the literature.
2. Databases included were Communication Abstracts; Communication Studies, Education, Health Sciences, Management and Organizational Studies, Political Science, Psychology, Sociology, and Urban Studies and Planning (SAGE Full-Text Collections); ERIC; FRANCIS; PAIS International; PsycARTICLES; PsycBOOKS; Social Services Abstracts; Sociological Abstracts; and Worldwide Political Science Abstracts.

References

Alkin, M. C. "Introduction." In T. Kellaghan and D. L. Stufflebeam (eds.), *International Handbook of Educational Evaluation. Part One: Perspectives.* Dordrecht, Netherlands: Kluwer Academic, 2003.

Alkin, M. C., and Taut, S. "Unbundling Evaluation Use." *Studies in Educational Evaluation,* 2003, *29,* 1–12.

Bandura, A. *Social Foundations of Thought and Action: A Social Cognitive Theory.* Upper Saddle River, N.J.: Prentice Hall, 1986.

Bouchard, S., and Cyr, C. *Recherche Psychosociale: Pour Harmoniser Recherche et Pratique.* Sainte-Foy (QC): Presses de l'Université du Québec, 1998.

Brett, B., Hill-Mead, L., and Wu, S. "Perspectives on Evaluation Use and Demand by Users: The Case of City Year." In V. J. Caracelli and H. Preskill (eds.), *The Expanding Scope of Evaluation Use. New Directions for Evaluation,* no. 88. San Francisco: Jossey-Bass, 2000.

Brunner, I., and Guzman, A. "Participatory Evaluation: A Tool to Assess Projects and Empower People." In R. F. Conner, and M. Hendricks (eds.), *International Innovations in Evaluation Methodology.* San Francisco: Jossey-Bass, 1989.

Cohen, L., Manion, L., and Morrison, K. *Research Methods in Education* (5th ed.). New York: Routledge Falmer, 2000.

Cousins, J. B. "Principals' Use of Appraisal Data Concerning Their Own Performance." Unpublished doctoral dissertation, University of Toronto, Toronto, 1988.

Cousins, J. B. "Assessing Program Needs Using Participatory Evaluation: A Comparison of High and Marginal Success Cases." In J. B. Cousins and L. Earl (eds.), *Participatory Evaluation in Education: Studies in Evaluation Use and Organizational Learning.* London: Falmer, 1995.

Cousins, J. B., Donohue, J. J., and Bloom, G. A. "Collaborative Evaluation in North America: Evaluators' Self-Reported Opinions, Practices and Consequences." *Evaluation Practice,* 1993, *17*(3), 207–226.

Cousins, J. B., and Earl, L. M. "The Case for Participatory Research." *Educational Evaluation and Policy Analysis,* 1992, *14*(4), 397–418.

Cousins, J. B., Goh, S. C., Clark, S., and Lee, L. E. "Integrating Evaluation Inquiry into the Organizational Culture: A Review and Synthesis of the Knowledge Base." *Canadian Journal of Program Evaluation,* 2004, *19*(2), 99–141.

Cousins, J. B., and Leithwood, K. A. "Enhancing Knowledge Utilization as a Strategy for School Improvement." *Knowledge: Creation, Diffusion, Utilization,* 1993, *14*(3), 305–333.

Dunn, W. N., and Holtzner, B. "Knowledge in Society: Anatomy of an Emergent Field." *Knowledge in Society,* 1988, *1,* 6–26.

Fetterman, D. "Empowerment Evaluation: An Introduction to Theory and Practice." In D. Fetterman, S. J. Kafttarian, and A. Wandersman (eds.), *Empowerment Evaluation: Knowledge and Tools for Self-Assessment and Accountability.* Thousand Oaks, Calif.: Sage, 1996.

Fetterman, D. "Empowerment Evaluation: A Response to Patton and Scriven." *Evaluation Practice,* 1997, *18*(3), 253–266.

Fetterman, D. "Fetterman-House: A Process Use Distinction and a Theory." In C. A. Christie (ed.), *The Practice-Theory Relationship in Evaluation.* New Directions for Evaluation no. 97. San Francisco: Jossey-Bass, 2003.

Forss, K., Cracknell, B., and Samset, K. "Can Evaluation Help an Organization to Learn?" *Evaluation Review,* 1994, *18*(5), 574–591.

Forss, K., Rebien, C. C., and Carlsson, J. "Process Use of Evaluations: Types of Use That Precede Lessons Learned and Feedback." *Evaluation,* 2002, *8*(1), 29–45.

Fraenkel, J. R., and Wallen, N. E. *How to Design and Evaluate Research in Education* (5th ed.). New York: McGraw-Hill, 2003.

Garaway, G. B. "Participatory Evaluation." *Studies in Educational Evaluation,* 1995, *21,* 85–102.

Greene, J. C. "Stakeholder Utilization and Participation in Program Evaluation." *Evaluation Review,* 1988, *18,* 574–591.

Green, J., and Southard, M. "Participatory Approaches to Evaluation for Supporting School Management: Three Case Studies." Paper presented at the Annual Meeting of the American Educational Research Association, San Francisco, California, 1995.

Greenstein, T. N. *Methods of Family Research* (2nd ed.). Thousand Oaks, Calif.: Sage, 2006.

Henry, G. T., and Mark, M. M. "Toward an Agenda for Research on Evaluation." In C. A. Christie (ed.), *The Practice–Theory Relationship in Evaluation. New Directions for Evaluation*, no. 97. San Francisco: Jossey-Bass, 2003.

Huberman, M. "Steps Toward an Integrated Model of Research Utilization." *Knowledge: Creation, Diffusion, Utilization*, 1987, *8*, 586–611.

Kamm, B. J. "Building Organizational Learning and Evaluation Capacity: A Study of Process Use." *Dissertation Abstracts International*, 2004, *65*(11), 4071A. (UMI no. 3154944)

King, J. A., and Pechman, E. M. "Pinning a Wave to the Shore: Conceptualizing Evaluation Use in School Systems." *Educational Evaluation and Policy Analysis*, 1984, *6*(3), 241–251.

Kirkhart, K. E. "Reconceptualizing Evaluation Use: An Integrated Theory of Influence." In V. J. Caracelli and H. Preskill (eds.), *The Expanding Scope of Evaluation Use. New Directions for Evaluation*, no. 88. San Francisco: Jossey-Bass, 2000.

Lau, G., and LeMahieu, P. "Changing Roles: Evaluator and Teacher Collaborating in School Change." *Evaluation and Program Planning*, 1997, *20*(1), 7–15.

Levin, B. "Collaborative Research in and with Organizations." *Qualitative Studies in Education*, 1993, *6*, 331–340.

Louis, K. S., and Dentler, R. A. "Knowledge Use and School Improvement." *Curriculum Inquiry*, 1988, *18*(10), 33–62.

Mertens, D. M., Farley, J., Singleton, P., and Madison, A. "Diverse Voices in Evaluation Practice: Feminists, Minorities, and Persons with Disabilities." *Evaluation Practice*, 1994, *15*(2), 123–129.

Morabito, S. M. "Evaluator Roles and Strategies for Expanding Evaluation Process Influence." *American Journal of Evaluation*, 2002, *23*(3), 321–330.

Newman, D. L., and Cai, M. "Teacher Involvement in Program Evaluation and Evaluation Use: An Empirical Examination of the Participatory Evaluation Approach." A paper presented at the Annual Meeting of the American Evaluation Association in conjunction with the International Evaluation Conference, Vancouver, B.C., Canada, 1995.

Patton, M. Q. "Developmental Evaluation." *Evaluation Practice*, 1994, *15*(3), 311–319.

Patton, M. Q. *Utilization-Focused Evaluation* (3rd ed.). Thousand Oaks, Calif.: Sage, 1997.

Patton, M. Q. "Discovering Process Use." *Evaluation*, 1998, *4*, 225–233.

Preskill, H. "Evaluation's Role in Enhancing Organizational Learning: A Model for Practice." *Evaluation and Program Planning*, 1994, *17*(3), 291–297.

Preskill, H. "Process Use." In S. Mathison (ed.), *Encyclopedia of Evaluation*. Thousand Oaks, Calif.: Sage, 2005.

Preskill, H., and Caracelli, V. "Current and Developing Conceptions of Use: Evaluation Use TIG Survey Results." *Evaluation Practice*, 1997, *18*(3), 209–225.

Preskill, H., Zuckerman, B., and Matthews, B. "An Exploratory Study of Process Use: Findings and Implications for Future Research." *American Journal of Evaluation*, 2003, *24*(4), 423–442.

Russ-Eft, D., Atwood, R., and Egherman, T. "Use and Non-Use of Evaluation Results: Case Study of Environmental Influences in the Private Sector." *American Journal of Evaluation*, 2002, *23*(1), 19–31.

Shulha, L. M. "Evaluative Inquiry in University-School Professional Learning Partnerships." In V. J. Caracelli and H. Preskill (eds.), *The Expanding Scope of Evaluation Use. New Directions for Evaluation*, no. 88. San Francisco: Jossey-Bass, 2000.

Stockdill, S. H., Baizerman, M., and Compton, D. W. "Toward a Definition of the ECB Process: A Conversation with the ECB Literature." In D. W. Compton, M. Baizerman, and S. H. Stockdill (eds.), *The Art, Craft, and Science of Evaluation Capacity Building. New Directions for Evaluation*, no. 93. San Francisco: Jossey-Bass, 2002.

Taut, S. M. "Evaluation Use for Learning in an International Development Cooperation Organization: An Empirical Study of Process Use and Capacity Building in Self-Evaluation." *Dissertation Abstracts International*, 2005, 66(07), 2553A. (UMI no. 3181761)

Trochim, W.M.K. *Research Methods Knowledge Base* (Measurement Validity Types). Retrieved Aug. 24, 2006, from http://www.socialresearchmethods.net/kb/measval.htm.

Turnbull, B. "A Confirmatory Factor Analytic Model of Evaluation Use." *Canadian Journal of Program Evaluation*, 1998, 13(2), 75–87.

Turnbull, B. "The Mediating Effect of Participation Efficacy on Evaluation Use." *Evaluation and Program Planning*, 1999, 22, 131–140.

Weiss, C. H. "The Stakeholder Approach to Evaluation: Origins and Promise." In A. S. Bryk (ed.), *Stakeholder-Based Evaluation. New Directions for Program Evaluation*, no. 17. San Francisco: Jossey-Bass, 1983.

Whyte, W. F. (ed.). *Participatory Action Research*. Thousands Oaks, Calif.: Sage, 1990.

COURTNEY AMO is a graduate student in the Faculty of Education, University of Ottawa, Ottawa, Ontario, and manager, performance and evaluation, at the Social Sciences and Humanities Research Council of Canada, Ottawa.

J. BRADLEY COUSINS is a professor of educational administration in the Faculty of Education, University of Ottawa.

NEW DIRECTIONS FOR EVALUATION • DOI: 10.1002/ev

2

This chapter describes the results of an exploratory study that sought to understand what U.S. American Evaluation Association members think process use looks like in practice.

Evaluators' Descriptions of Process Use: An Exploratory Study

Michael A. Harnar, Hallie Preskill

In *Utilization Focused Evaluation* (1997), Patton introduced the term *process use* to describe changes in thinking and behavior, whether at the individual, program, or organizational level, as a result of one's participation in an evaluation, irrespective of the evaluation results. In conversations with stakeholders, Patton found that although stakeholders changed how they did their work after an evaluation was completed, they did not attribute these changes directly to the evaluation results. Rather, they credited the changes to their experience with the evaluation. In support of this new term, Patton proposed some indicators of process use: (1) enhancing shared understandings; (2) furthering the program intervention; (3) increasing engagement; and (4) program and organizational development.

Before Patton coined the term *process use,* the literature on use or utilization generally emphasized use of evaluation findings. For example, evaluation use has been described as encompassing (1) instrumental use, which occurs when the results are tangibly used to make programmatic improvements; (2) conceptual use, which suggests that people change their thinking or understanding (conceptual schema) about the program on the basis of the evaluation's findings; and (3) symbolic or persuasive use, which refers to the findings being used in symbolic or persuasive ways—for

Note: We would like to extend our gratitude and appreciation to Dreolin Fleischer for her willingness to let us add our research question to her master's thesis research study, and for making her data available to us for inclusion in this chapter.

example, to lobby for resources, or to show that the program has met its evaluation obligations (Weiss, 1998). While these terms enjoy a solid place in the lexicon of the evaluation field, less has been written about the construct of process use.

The idea that stakeholders are affected by their participation in an evaluation is not new. Numerous articles prior to Patton's explication (1997) of process use have focused on the topic of stakeholder involvement and learning (for example, Cousins and Leithwood, 1993; Cousins, Donohue, and Bloom, 1996; Forss, Cracknell, and Samset, 1994; King and Pechman, 1984; Preskill, 1994; Preskill and Preskill, 1997). An excellent analysis of this literature is discussed by Amo and Cousins (Chapter One of this volume), where they categorize and describe eighteen studies conducted on topics related to process use. However, since 1997 an increasing number of studies have focused on and used the term *process use*. That is, they have looked specifically at how and what stakeholders learn from their involvement in the evaluation process (Forss, Rebien, and Carlsson, 2002; Kamm, 2004; Preskill, Zuckerman, and Matthews, 2003; Russ-Eft, Atwood, and Egherman, 2002; Shulha, 2000; Sutherland, 2004; Taut, 2005). Though each of these studies included its own population, used a variety of research designs and methods, and operationalized the construct of process use in its own way, they all concluded that stakeholders learned something from their engagement in the evaluation process. This learning was at the individual, group, or organization level and was related to development of new knowledge, attitudes, or behaviors.

Interest in what stakeholders learn from their engagement in an evaluation may be a result of the convergence of several events and trends in the evaluation field. The first might be Patton's book (1997) in which he defined and discussed process use, which became a catalyst for the use of the term. Another might be the 2000 and 2001 themes of the American Evaluation Association conferences, which were Evaluation Capacity Building and Mainstreaming Evaluation, bringing attention to the need to involve stakeholders in evaluations in substantive ways. A third trend is the increasing commitment to involving stakeholders in evaluation. In their study on evaluation use a decade ago, Preskill and Caracelli (1997) found that 80 percent of their survey's respondents agreed that evaluators should take responsibility for involving stakeholders in evaluation processes. Fleischer (2007) asked the same question on her iteration of the evaluation use survey and found that 98 percent agreed with this assertion. Consequently, one might conclude that stakeholder involvement in evaluation, at least to some degree, has become commonplace in evaluation practice.

The increasing involvement of stakeholders in evaluation processes and the growing research base on process use led us to wonder what evaluators thought process use looked like. Though the term is now ten years old, we have sensed that the construct may not be fully understood or known by many evaluation practitioners. For example, from their study of process use Forss, Rebien, and Carlsson (2002) concluded, "We do not doubt that process use exists, but we do not know how common it is. . . . There is a need to know more about process use, and to verify whether it occurs as often as some like to believe it does" (p. 43). Amo and Cousins (in this volume) conclude that there is a "paucity of empirical studies examining the concept of process use directly or indirectly. Almost a decade after coining the concept, there is still much opportunity to study, question, probe, test, and substantiate process use" (p. 20). As we reflected on this research and our own experiences, we began to wonder about the extent to which evaluation practitioners knew about and understood the term *process use*. Thus, the purpose of our research was to explore the question, "What does process use look like to evaluators?" Our hope is that the results of this exploratory study will help further clarify and operationalize the construct, which can then be useful in informing future education, training, and research on the topic of process use.

Methods

To address the research question "What does process use look like?" a question was designed and included as part of a larger study on evaluation use conducted by Fleischer (2007). Fleischer's study was a follow up to a survey conducted by Preskill and Caracelli (1997) that sought to understand how members of the Evaluation Use Topical Interest Group of the American Evaluation Association perceived evaluation use relative to designing and implementing evaluations. Keeping many of the items from the 1997 survey, Fleischer also added several new questions and allowed the authors of this article to include one open-ended question on process use. Her survey addressed these topics: professional identity (three items), perceptions of the current field of evaluation (twelve), the role of the evaluator (ten), factors that increase evaluation use (fifteen), stakeholder involvement (seven), the role of evaluation in fostering organizational outcomes (ten), background information (five), and our question on process use (one).

Designed as a Web-based survey, an invitation to participate in the study was sent via email to 3,824 AEA members in the United States. Usable responses were received from 1,140 individuals (30 percent response rate). Table 2.1 shows the survey respondents' characteristics.

Of the respondents, 481 (42 percent) wrote something in response to the question "Reflecting on your own evaluation experience and practice, what does process use look like?" This question was placed prior to the final set of demographic items and after sections on evaluation use and evaluation misuse. To contextualize the use and misuse sections, definitions of *evaluation findings* and *evaluation process use* were put at the beginning of the section on evaluation use. This is the definition of process use provided:

> Refers to cognitive, behavioral, program and organizational changes resulting from engagement in the evaluation process and learning to think evaluatively (for example, goals clarification, conceptualizing the program's logic model,

Table 2.1. Demographics of Survey Respondents (n = 1,140)

Characteristics	Percentage
Professional identity	
—Evaluation is my primary professional identity.	51
—Evaluation is my secondary professional identity after another discipline.	45
—Evaluation is not part of my professional identity.	4
Evaluator's role	
—I conduct evaluations primarily where evaluation services are external to the organization.	37
—I conduct evaluations primarily where evaluation services are internal to the organization.	22
—I conduct primarily a mix of both internal and external evaluation.	33
—I am not currently conducting evaluations.	8
Experience level	
—A relative beginner	13
—At an intermediate level	44
—At an advanced level	43
Number of years conducting evaluations	
—Less than five	29
—6–10	28
—11–20	24
—20 or more	19

identifying evaluation priorities, struggling with measurement issues, participation in design and interpretation). Process use occurs when those involved in the evaluation learn from the evaluation process itself or make program changes based on the evaluation process rather than findings—as, for example, when those involved in the evaluation later say "the impact on our program came not just from the findings but also from going through the thinking process that the evaluation required" [Patton, personal communication].

Patton offered this definition to Fleischer for her survey. A similar definition debuted in *Utilization Focused Evaluation* (UFE) (1997), and another will be in Patton's fourth edition of the UFE book (in press).

To consider any nonresponse error (Dillman, 2000), we looked at descriptive statistics on a sample of relevant items to identify any differences in those who did (n = 481) and did not (n = 659) respond to the open-ended question on process use. Nearly all of the analyses showed that both groups were relatively similar in how they responded to each of the survey items; percentages were generally within one or two percentage points and mean scores were within one or two tenths of a point on a five-point Likert-type scale. Given the apparent similarity between these two groups, no further comparative analyses were conducted. However, a few items did illustrate some differences between the two groups and are worth noting. Specifically, those who responded to the process use question had more years of experience conducting evaluations ($\chi^2(3, N = 1016) = 12.405, p = .006$) and tended to identify their level of evaluation knowledge and experience as "advanced" ($\chi^2(2, N = 1135) = 14.279, p = .001$).

The other difference was found in respondents' answers to the question about choosing which of several evaluation approaches are most important in the field of evaluation. When comparing those who did and did not respond to the process use question, we found that those who gave a response were more likely to identify participatory, user-focused, social-justice or democratic, and evaluation-for-capacity-building approaches as more important than objectives-based, theory-driven, experimental or quasiexperimental, and empowerment approaches to evaluation ($\chi^2(7, N = 1102) = 14.888, p = .037$; see Table 2.2).

We will speculate later, in the Discussion section, what these differences might mean in light of our findings from the responses to the process-use question.

Data Analysis

The 481 responses to the open-ended question on process use were sent to the authors in a Microsoft Excel file and then imported into a qualitative analysis software program (Atlas.ti). As we studied the data, we realized that both the respondents' clarity and our conceptual clarity about what process use looks like were much fuzzier than anticipated. To understand, interpret, and ultimately draw conclusions from the respondents' answers, we used an inductive coding process (Patton, 2002) to increase the validity of our interpretations.

Table 2.2. Most Important Evaluation Approaches of Responders and Nonresponders to the Process Use Question

Evaluation Approach	Responders (n = 474)	Nonresponders (n = 628)
User-focused	112 (23%)	123 (20%)
Objectives-based	107 (23%)	157 (25%)
Participatory	81 (17%)	74 (12%)
Evaluation for capacity building	51 (11%)	62 (10%)
Theory-driven	46 (10%)	76 (12%)
Experimental or quasiexperimental	44 (9%)	83 (13%)
Empowerment evaluation	18 (3%)	34 (5%)
Social justice and democratic	15 (3%)	19 (3%)

1. Independently, we each read the first two pages of the twenty-four-page document (481 responses) to become familiar with the data—to "see what was there." Together, we discussed emerging themes and arrived at a list of categories and codes that resulted in two broad categories of process use: activities and outcomes. Within each of these categories, we identified a series of subcategories and related codes.
2. Independently, we used these codes to analyze all the responses. Together, we then went through every response and shared our coding. Where there were differences, we discussed how we interpreted the response and negotiated the resulting category assignment (code). This process clarified and made more concrete the various terms respondents used.
3. We then printed out each category of responses and individually read through the categories to determine if they were coded accurately. During this process, we also refined the category labels. As we read through the data one last time to develop our interpretations, we made a few final coding changes.

This intensive process gave us a fair amount of confidence in understanding what the respondents communicated with regard to process use.

Findings

Survey respondents were asked to describe, in their own words, the answer to the question, "Reflecting on your own evaluation experience and practice, what does process use look like?" During the coding process, we found a number of responses that did not fit with the emergent categorical framework. Some respondents mentioned not understanding the question (n = 26), not knowing what process use is (n = 14), and never having seen or experienced it (n = 11). However, the majority of responses in this category (n = 85) were either difficult to interpret (regardless of any framework) or were metaphorical, thus limiting our ability to speculate on what the author actually meant. We discuss this group of responses later, but first we report on the remaining 345 responses that more clearly addressed our research question.

The majority of evaluators who responded to this question tended to talk about process use as something that happens during the evaluation process or as an outcome of having engaged in an evaluation. A smaller percentage described it as evaluation being embedded in work practices, as learning or change, and as evaluation capacity building. The next section describes these findings in more detail.

The Evaluation Process. Of the 345 responses, more than half (n = 195 of 345, 57 percent) described process use as being engaged in evaluation processes. Two themes emerged in this category of responses. The first has to do with stakeholder involvement. Slightly more than one third (n = 136 of 345, 39 percent) of all respondents depicted process use as involving stakeholders in some aspect of an evaluation's design or implementation. Their responses positioned the evaluator as a facilitator who uses a collaborative, participatory approach and is committed to an open, engaged process with ongoing communication.

> Involvement of stakeholders, staff, consumers, and others in the planning and implementation of evaluation.

> Process use looks like stakeholders and evaluators collaborating throughout the evaluation activities.

> Involving stakeholders in verifying conclusions and recommendations of study/evaluation results. Clarifying implications of evaluation results so that stakeholders can make informed decisions about next steps or new directions to take.

> Involving stakeholders in the initial design of the evaluative process, in the development of a logic model that will guide the evaluative process.

> Process use can be the most exciting aspect of evaluation when stakeholders in the organization are involved from the beginning.

Of those who talked about engaging stakeholders in the evaluation process (n = 136), slightly more than one third described process use as when the evaluator intentionally employs various learning processes (n = 53 of 136, 39 percent). As seen in a number of quotes, these learning processes include (1) asking questions; (2) engaging in dialogue; (3) reflection, critical, or evaluative thinking; (4) exploring assumptions; and (5) giving and receiving feedback.

> Staff gain insight about their own assumptions and attain higher levels of clarity about why they do what they do the way they do it. They become more precise and gain a sense that they have a right to take a time out and reflect. They also engage in conversations with one another that they would not otherwise do and develop a more powerful collective identification.

> Process use involves getting programs staff and managers to acknowledge and question the assumptions surrounding their programs. It provides them an opportunity to look at their program analytically and, to a certain extent, objectively to facilitate solutions to problems.

> In initially designing the evaluation, staff and stakeholders usually reexamine assumptions about the best outcomes and indicators and feasible methods of collecting related data. Sometimes, these realizations occur during or following collection of data.

NEW DIRECTIONS FOR EVALUATION • DOI: 10.1002/ev

Inviting people into critical, evaluative thinking can help them to view their intentions and programs from new, unexpected, and valuable perspectives.

Process use looks like learning through doing (procedural knowledge). Often stakeholders come to the experience with no real idea of the role of evaluation. When they participate in the process, they leave with new perceptions and/or intellectual skills for thinking critically about their program(s). Process use looks like looking through *new* glasses at their program(s).

Of those who responded to the process use question, 17 percent (n = 59 of 345; Table 2.3) described process use as the *process of evaluation*. However, these respondents were not clear about who was involved in the evaluation process. As such, they may have been suggesting that process use is what happens during the process of an evaluation and were describing the phases or activities of an evaluation's design and implementation:

Evaluation process meetings are often the only times organizations pause to consider their goals and objectives, try to operationalize those, consider what success or effectiveness really means. In my setting the process is often started very early.

Consistent use of methodology relevant to the question at hand. Appropriate use of human subjects. Accurate reporting of data and findings.

I'm not quite certain what is meant here. I consider the evaluation "problem" and adjust processes to achieve evaluation goals. There is not one process I use.

Looking at the various processes . . . to achieve results and analyzing those processes.

Evaluation process is describing the project, defining the project goals, deciding on the methodology, analyzing the data, and reporting the result. If I understand your question of process use, this is what I follow and use for evaluation.

Three of the 345 respondents (< 1 percent) described process use as process evaluation—collecting information on a program's processes.

Outcomes of Stakeholder Engagement in the Evaluation Process. Just over one third of the respondents identified process use as an outcome of stakeholders' involvement in the evaluation process (n = 118 of 345, 34 percent). These individuals seemed to suggest that involving stakeholders in an evaluation leads to process use. Process use results in either changes in stakeholders' perspectives about their program or evaluation in general or changes in their program.

Table 2.3. Summary of Responses for Each Category (n = 345)

Category	N	Percentage
Evaluation process	195	57
—Stakeholder involvement	136	39
—Used learning processes	53	15
—Process of evaluation	59	17
Process evaluation	3	<1
Outcomes of stakeholder engagement in evaluation process	118	34
—Change in perspective about evaluation	27	8
—Change in perspective about program	44	13
—Program improvement, formative evaluation	47	14
Embedded in daily work practices	38	11
Individual, group, organizational learning, and change	22	6
Evaluation capacity building	5	1

Note: The number of codings sums to more than 481 (100 percent) because some respondents' answers addressed more than one theme. There was an occasion for instance, when one person mentioned both a process and an outcome. We parsed one from the other and coded each separately. Although a total response may have received more than one code, no idea was double-coded.

Of the 118 respondents who described process use as an outcome, 44 (37 percent) reported that process use led to stakeholders gaining a better understanding of their program.

> Clients who say, "Now that I've been through the evaluation technical assistance process, I understand what my program does, and how we do it."

> Process use often emerges as an "aha" moment where an intended user sees her program from a different perspective and is motivated to make changes in her work or even her attitude about her work based on that moment of awareness.

> I see program staff better able to articulate their program model and understand the possible links between their interventions and the expected outcomes. They are better able to design future interventions as a result of involvement in the evaluation process.

> We regularly see clients and program stakeholders develop an ability to write and use more appropriate statements of goals and objectives; embrace strategies for multiple/varied uses of evaluation results; and learn to align program input, process, products, and outcomes using logic models, which they go on to apply to later programs.

Twenty-seven (23 percent) of the 118 respondents who described process use as an outcome suggested that stakeholders' involvement in the evaluation process often leads to change in their perspective about evaluation. They believe that stakeholders may gain evaluation knowledge and skills, develop new understanding about how evaluation applies to their program, and begin to value evaluation. Though evaluation is not necessarily embedded in their daily practice, they do think more critically about their program and now view their programs through a more evaluative lens.

> The evaluation process often produces the result of program staff members developing a better understanding of the evaluation process and how and why things are done in a certain way.

> Once stakeholders experience and understand the evaluation process, they identify additional evaluation questions and future needs.

> Although many will not become evaluators themselves, they do become intelligent consumers of evaluation information.

> After the evaluation is completed, they are able to understand how to think like an evaluator and determine what questions they want to ask next and how to do it.

> Organizations become savvier about knowing which data to ask for and how to use them.

Another outcome of stakeholder involvement in the evaluation process, described by 47 of the 118 respondents (40 percent) is when stakeholders use what they learn from the evaluation to make program improvements (formative evaluation, instrumental use). Of particular interest was how many discussed using findings prior to completion of the evaluation. In other words, process use describes stakeholders applying their learning as it occurs rather than waiting for the evaluation to be completely finished.

> Stakeholders involved in implementing evaluation and making formative use of interim findings.

> Learning and the resulting organizational and programmatic changes that happen prior to completion of reporting data.

> Incremental changes during the evaluation process.

> Stakeholders carefully reviewing the evaluation results and discussing the results, and modifying programs accordingly.

> An amazing amount of information comes to light in the course of an evaluation, and changes are made in the normal course of business based on what

has been learned. The day-to-day formative decisions and learning do not wait until the final product has been received and reviewed, though summative decisions may require the final report to implement the decision.

Evaluation Embedded into the Daily Routine. Eleven percent (n = 38 of 345) of the respondents described process use as when evaluation is integrated into the ongoing, daily work of the program. This occurs as organization members consistently take opportunities to engage in evaluating their programs:

> Integration of findings and procedures into the regular decision-making and improvement of program functioning, with an emphasis on enhancing program outcomes.

> Seamlessly integrating systematic data collection into the ongoing monitoring and oversight functions of an organization.

> The clients report they are able to do it themselves; evaluation becomes part of their own professional and organizational context.

> Successful evaluation process use is when the evaluation steps become a regular/accepted part of program/initiative operation.

> People thinking evaluatively, asking evaluative questions, raising questions about assumptions, and incorporating evaluative thinking into discussions and decision making.

Individual, Group, and Organizational Learning and Change. For 6 percent of the respondents (n = 22 of 345), process use specifically looks like individual, group, and organizational learning and change.

> Process use "looks like" a change process. The very act of being immersed in evaluation changes me as a person and changes the programs I am involved with.

> Organizational learning and discovery through the steps of gathering and providing information and materials needed for the evaluation.

> Outstanding process use will *always* foster organization learning.

> Process use is identified during and after the evaluation when an individual verbalizes how he or she now views the organization and what was learned through the process.

Evaluation Capacity Building. Five respondents (n = 5 of 345, 1 percent) referred to process use as evaluation capacity building (ECB).

These responses primarily focused on training or teaching others about evaluation.

> Training clients to do or frame their own evaluations.

> We occasionally conduct evaluation capacity building workshops for new project directors (typically small nonprofits or community groups), and we consistently receive feedback (formal and informal) which indicates that participants consider the processes (for example, using a logic model to outline their program, formulating evaluation questions, designing an evaluation for their program) to be valuable for gaining greater clarity about their program activities and goals.

> For the most part, similar to evaluation capacity building.

Miscellaneous Responses. As mentioned earlier, more than a quarter of the responses (n = 136 of 481, 28 percent) were coded as "miscellaneous" (see Table 2.4). Our emergent categorical framework was built around the explicit meaning in the responses. Every effort was made to avoid interpreting the responses beyond their manifest content. Neither of us allowed the other to make assumptions in discerning what the respondent meant with an answer. For this reason, many of the responses in this category challenged us in gleaning their meaning, and after much debate we coded them "miscellaneous."

Miscellaneous-coded responses included respondents saying they (1) had never seen process use (n = 11, 2 percent), (2) did not know what process use was (n = 14, 3 percent), or (3) did not understand the question (n = 26, 5 percent). Another group gave responses (1) whose meaning was difficult to discern, (2) where it was unclear how the response was related to process use, or (3) that were metaphorical (n = 85, 18 percent). Here are some of their answers:

> Have never seen process use ("I can't name a single process use in over twenty years as a practicing evaluator"; "I don't really have enough experience to paint a good picture of process use in evaluation practice"; "I wish I could say that I've seen it!")

Table 2.4. Miscellaneous Responses (n = 136) and Percentage of the Total Responses (n = 481)

Category	n	%
Have not seen or experienced process use	11	2
Said they did not know what process use was	14	3
Said they did not understand the question	26	5
Unclear meaning unrelated to question, metaphorical	85	18

NEW DIRECTIONS FOR EVALUATION • DOI: 10.1002/ev

Did not know what process use was ("I don't understand what you mean by "process use"; "I am not as familiar with this approach"; "I am not familiar with what you mean by process use. Evaluation process use?")

Did not understand the question ("Sorry I do not know what you are asking here."; "I don't understand the sort of response you're looking for here")

Difficult to discern meaning or relationship to process use; metaphorical ("I suspect that it is largely invisible like air. I am not sure that most users are consciously aware of it"; "About 75 percent of clients will take it as constructive and about 25 percent are looking for a preconceived outcome"; "Users have a selective memory on unfavorable findings"; "Sausage making, but the product can be tasty"; "Everyday stuff")

We consider why such a large number of individuals gave what we considered unusable responses in the next section.

Discussion

Our aim in this exploratory study was to learn what evaluators think process use looks like in their practice. Our question, "Reflecting on your own evaluation experience and practice, what does process use look like?" was placed in an evaluation use survey that was sent to all U.S.-based AEA members. Of the 3,824 people invited to participate, 1,140 completed the survey (30 percent response rate). Of those, 481 individuals answered our question on process use (42 percent of the survey's respondents).

In terms of who responded to the process use question as opposed to those who did not, we noted a few differences. Generally, respondents to the process-use question were more experienced evaluators who chose as most important participatory, user-focused, social-justice democratic, or ECB approaches. We might speculate that these respondents are more, rather than less, familiar with the concept of process use because these evaluation approaches tend to include stakeholders in the evaluation process, where learning from an evaluation is implied, if not specifically intentional.

Given that the data represent the responses to a single open-ended item on a rather lengthy survey, one must be careful in generalizing from the findings of this study. However, we believe the results permit some interesting and valuable insights into what evaluators know and believe about process use. First, a large proportion of respondents (39 percent) clearly view process use as related to stakeholder involvement in the evaluation process, which directly reflects Patton's definition of process use. This finding is particularly interesting in light of the results from Fleischer's survey (2007). When asked to rate the extent to which they agree that evaluators should take responsibility for "involving stakeholders in the evaluation process" (on a five-point Likert-type scale, 5 = strongly agree), the mean response was 4.7 (SD = .542).

Next, we found that for many, process use is what happens *during* the process of an evaluation (57 percent). Respondents discussed engaging stakeholders in a variety of evaluation activities. They included simply meeting with one or more stakeholders to determine the purpose of the evaluation and possible key questions, or more fully engaging stakeholders in designing and implementing data collection methods and instruments, analyzing data, and developing recommendations. This depth of participation reflects one of five dimensions Weaver and Cousins (2003; developed from Cousins and Whitmore, 1998) use to describe the process of collaborative forms of inquiry. This finding suggests that evaluators view process use as something that occurs during the evaluation process, but they did not describe the changes or learning that might occur during the evaluation process (as indicated in Patton's definition), instead merely describing their own evaluation methods and processes.

We also found that 34 percent of the respondents discussed process use as an outcome (change in perspective about their programs, change in attitude toward evaluation, or stakeholders making programmatic improvements). This set of responses appears congruent with Patton's definition of process use: "Refers to cognitive, behavioral, program and organizational changes resulting from engagement in the evaluation process and learning to think evaluatively."

We also found it intriguing that less than 1 percent (n = 5 of 345) of the respondents discussed process use as involving stakeholders for the purpose of evaluation capacity building, and 6 percent (n = 22 of 345) talked about process use as relating to individual, group, and organizational learning. We expected more to have mentioned capacity building and learning in their responses given the definition's emphasis on learning and change. In other words, few people talked about process use as something that is intentionally built into the evaluation process. Although Preskill, Zuckerman, and Matthews (2003) recommended that evaluators be intentional about process use, after reflecting more on Patton's definition, our own work on evaluation capacity building, and the answers provided by the survey respondents, we now agree with Forss, Rebien, and Carlsson (2002), who suggested that the learnings from stakeholder engagement "reside in the process of evaluation, and they occur as a *side effect* of this unfolding process" (italics added for emphasis; p. 43). Consequently, we believe that process use is more reflective of incidental or informal learning—a by-product that occurs from stakeholders' engagement in the evaluation (an outcome)—while ECB represents the evaluator's clear intentions to build learning into the evaluation process (Elkjaer and Wahlgren, 2006; Marsick and Watkins, 1990, 1997; Preskill and Boyle, 2007). Such a process includes identifying specific expected individual, group, and organizational outcomes, as well as using facilitative learning processes throughout the evaluation (Preskill and Torres, 1999). Support for highlighting the intentionality of ECB can be seen in the definition of ECB offered by Stockdill, Baizerman, and Compton (2002), who write that ECB is "the intentional work to continuously create and sustain overall organizational processes that make quality evaluation and its uses routine" (p. 14). It should be noted, however, that stakeholder involvement in an evaluation is only one of several strategies that can be used to build evaluation capacity (Preskill and Boyle, 2007). Though Patton has often implied that process use is intentional, as in "intended use for intended users," we do not think this expectation is particularly explicit in his definition. Given recent conceptual thinking and research on ECB, it is possible that these two constructs are related but different and would be better understood along a continuum of intentionality (Preskill and Boyle, 2007).

We were somewhat surprised that 28 percent of the respondents offered a description of process use that has little to do with how the term is defined. This was unexpected given that the definition was encountered just two computer screens earlier. Placement of the definition lends some credibility to the responses we could decipher, but it implies that a substantial number of evaluators were not able to articulate what process use looks like even after they are told what it is. This may imply a lack of understanding of what the term means, or that they did not read or understand the question, or that it may be an artifact of the question itself. Although we worked hard to ensure that the question would elicit respondents' perceptions of process use, we are open to the possibility that some respondents found the question difficult to interpret.

At the same time, framing this question as an effort at construct validation, this study could be thought of as an application test. Generally, construct validation aims to establish agreement on the existence of a psychological concept (Crano and Brewer, 2002). If the construct does exist, then one's interpretation of it should predictably relate to interpretations of other constructs (convergent and discriminant validity). A natural next step, after convergent and discriminant validity checks, is application of the construct. We asked people to read a definition, assimilate the information, and then describe an application of the definition. It may be that this effort is too advanced a procedure for this construct; long-held constructs, such as validity or reliability, are probably much easier to interpret and apply. Attempts at construct validation involving discriminating process use from other evaluation terms may be more appropriate at this stage of the construct's life. Future research might involve scenario-based exercises in which people are asked to identify process use, or items that ask respondents to differentiate between process use and other use-related constructs. Such efforts would likely help to further understand the meaning and use of this construct and how we might distinguish it from other constructs.

Implications for Research and the Evaluation Field. There is a strong trend in the evaluation community toward involving stakeholders in the evaluation process. The consequence of this involvement is, therefore, an important research topic. Whereas existing research supports the fact that changes in individuals, groups, and organizations occur as a result of their participation in an evaluation, the results of this exploratory study lend some support to our belief that the term and underlying construct of process use still need further development and articulation. To proceed in validating this construct, evaluation researchers should focus on how process use interacts with and against other constructs within the use schema. For instance, researchers might explore (1) the variables that affect changes in stakeholders' behavior and thinking as a result of engagement in the evaluation; (2) how the depth, scope, and breadth of stakeholder involvement affects changes in their thinking and behavior; and (3) the relationship between process use and evaluation capacity building. Evaluation theorists might also consider the extent to which various evaluation approaches contribute to or facilitate process use.

With regard to the usefulness of the term *process use* (which was the catalyst for the first author's interest in this study), we believe more discussion is needed. From the results of this study, we question whether the term is confusing to many evaluators, given that the field uses the term *process* in describing the process *of* evaluation and process evaluations. At the same time, we do think process use is occurring as suggested by the respondents' descriptions of the term. Given the fact that most respondents discussed or implied stakeholder involvement in the evaluation process, process use can be considered a natural by-product of such engagement. More conceptual thinking about this construct is warranted given the results of this study. We also suggest that if stakeholder learning is the desired outcome, and learning is intentional from the beginning of the evaluation, then this should be called ECB. Therefore, research on how to translate process use into ECB would further the field's understanding of these two critically important but underdeveloped constructs.

References

Cousins, J. B. "Utilization Effects of Participatory Evaluation." In T. Kellaghan and D. L. Stufflebeam (eds.), *International Handbook of Educational Evaluation*. Dordrecht, Netherlands: Kluwer Academic, 2003.

Cousins, J. B., Donohue, J. J., and Bloom, G. A. "Collaborative Evaluation in North America: Evaluators' Self-Reported opinions, Practices, and Consequences." *Evaluation Practice*, 1996, 17(3), 207–226.

Cousins, J. B., and Leithwood, K. A. "Enhancing Knowledge Utilization as a Strategy for School Improvement." *Knowledge: Creation, Diffusion, Utilization*, 1993, 14(3), 305–333.

Cousins, J. B., and Whitmore, E. "Framing Participatory Evaluation." In E. Whitmore (ed.), *Understanding and Practicing Participatory Evaluation. New Directions for Evaluation*, no. 80. San Francisco: Jossey-Bass, 1998.

Crano, W. D., and Brewer, M. B. *Principles and Methods of Social Research* (2nd ed.). Mahwah, N.J.: Erlbaum, 2002.

Dillman, D. A. *Mail and Internet Surveys: The Tailored Design Method* (2nd ed.). New York: Wiley, 2000.

Elkjaer, B., and Wahlgren, B. "Organizational Learning and Workplace Learning: Similarities and Differences." In E. Antonacopoulou, P. Jarvis, V. Anderson, B. Elkjaer, and S. Hoyrup (eds.), *Learning, Working, and Living: Mapping the Terrain of Working Life Learning.* New York: Palgrave Macmillan, 2006.

Fleischer, D. "Evaluation Use: A Survey of U.S. American Evaluation Association Members." Unpublished master's thesis, Claremont Graduate University, 2007.

Forss, K., Cracknell, B., and Samset, K. (1994). "Can Evaluation Help an Organization to Learn?" *Evaluation Review,* 1994, *18*(5), 574–591.

Forss, K., Rebien, C. C., and Carlsson, J. Process Use of Evaluations. *Evaluation,* 2002, *8*(1), 29–45.

Henry, G. "Why Not Use?" In V. J. Caracelli and H. Preskill (eds.), *The Expanding Scope of Evaluation Use. New Directions for Evaluation,* no. 88. San Francisco: Jossey-Bass, 2000.

King, J. A., and Pechman, E. M. "Pinning a Wave to the Shore: Conceptualizing Evaluation Use in School Systems." *Educational Evaluation and Policy Analysis,* 1984, *6*(3), 241–251.

Kamm, B. L. *Building Organizational Learning and Evaluation Capacity: A Study of Process Use.* Dissertation Abstracts Iternational, (UMI No. 3154944), 2004.

Marsick, V. J., and Watkins, K. E. *Informal and Incidental Learning in the Workplace.* London: Routledge, 1990.

Marsick, V. J., and Watkins, K. E. "Lessons from Informal and Incidental Learning." In J. Burgoyne and M. Reynolds (eds.), *Management Learning; Integrating Perspectives in Theory and Practice.* London: Sage, 1997.

Patton, M. Q. *Utilization-Focused Evaluation: The New Century Text* (3rd ed.). Thousand Oaks, Calif.: Sage, 1997.

Patton, M. Q. *Qualitative Research and Evaluation Methods* (3rd ed.). Thousand Oaks, Calif.: Sage, 2002.

Patton, M. Q. *Utilization-Focused Evaluation* (4th ed.). Thousand Oaks, Calif.: Sage, in press.

Preskill, H. "Evaluation's Role in Facilitating Organizational Learning: A Model for Practice." *Evaluation and Program Planning,* 1994, *17,* 291–298.

Preskill, H., and Boyle, S. "Building Evaluation Capacity: A Framework for Design and Implementation." Paper presented at the Canadian Evaluation Society annual conference, Winnipeg, Manitoba, June 2007.

Preskill, H., and Caracelli, V. "Current and Developing Conceptions of Use: Evaluation Use TIG Survey Results." *Evaluation Practice,* 1997, *18,* 209–225.

Preskill, S. L., and Preskill, H. "Meeting the Postmodern Challenge: Pragmatism and Evaluative Inquiry for Organizational Learning." *Advances in Program Evaluation,* 1997, *3,* 155–169.

Preskill, H., and Torres, R. T. *Evaluative Inquiry for Learning in Organizations.* Thousand Oaks, Calif.: Sage, 1999.

Preskill, H., Zuckerman, B., and Matthews, B. "An Exploratory Study of Process Use: Findings and Implications for Future Research." *American Journal of Evaluation,* 2003, *24*(4), 423–442.

Russ-Eft, D., Atwood, R., and Egherman, T. "Use and Non-Use of Evaluation Results: Case Studies of Environmental Influences in the Private Sector." *American Journal of Evaluation,* 2002, *23*(1), 19–31.

Shulha, L. "Evaluative Inquiry in University-School Professional Learning Partnerships." *New Directions for Evaluation,* no. 88, 2000.

Stockdill, S., Baizerman, M., and Compton, D. W. "Toward a Definition of the ECB Process: A Conversation with the Literature." In D. Compton, M. Baizerman, and S. H. Stockdill (eds.), *The Art, Craft and Science of Evaluation Capacity Building. New Directions for Evaluation,* no. 93. San Francisco: Jossey-Bass, 2002.

Sutherland, S. "Creating a Culture of Data Use for Continuous Improvement: A Case Study of an Edison School Project." *American Journal of Evaluation*, 2004, *25*(3) 277–293.

Taut, S. M. *Evaluation Use for Learning in an International Development Cooperation Organization: An Empirical Study of Process Use and Capacity Building in Self-evaluation.* Dissertation Abstracts International (UMI No. 3181761).

Weaver, L., and Cousins, J. B. "Unpacking the Participatory Process." *Journal of Multidisciplinary Evaluation*, 2004, *1*, 19–40.

Weiss, C. H. "Have We Learned Anything New About the Use of Evaluation?" *American Journal of Evaluation*, 1998, *19*, 21–33.

MICHAEL A. HARNAR is a Ph.D. student in the Evaluation and Applied Research Methods program in the School of Behavioral and Organizational Sciences at Claremont Graduate University.

HALLIE PRESKILL is a professor in the School of Behavioral and Organizational Sciences at Claremont Graduate University.

3

Over time, intentional process use can have the practical effect of building the evaluation capacity of an organization. This chapter outlines possible steps that take purposeful advantage of the evaluation process.

Developing Evaluation Capacity Through Process Use

Jean A. King

"Good, quick, cheap: pick two." This hackneyed evaluator's saw, borrowed from the restaurant industry, reminds us that in an organizational world where *good* is demanded and *cheap* is necessary, *quick* often has to go. My work in the past decade with organizations—many of which lack sufficient resources for program evaluation—has required me, working collaboratively with staff, to develop high-quality, affordable evaluation practices that are sustainable internally over time. Enter process use. Without knowing it, for almost thirty years I have engaged in and fostered process use during program evaluations in a range of educational and social service settings. Like Monsieur Jourdain, the hero of Molière's "Le Bourgeois Gentilhomme," who was pleased to learn that he had been speaking prose his entire life, I now have a label for this aspect of my evaluation practice, which is implicit in earlier writing (for example, King and Pechman, 1984; King, 1988).

This chapter discusses how to make process use an independent variable in evaluation practice: the purposeful means of building an organization's capacity to conduct and use evaluations in the long run. The goal of evaluation capacity building (ECB) is to strengthen and sustain effective program evaluation practices through a number of activities: (1) increasing an organization's capacity to design, implement, and manage effective evaluation projects; (2) accessing, building, and using evaluative knowledge and skills; (3) cultivating a spirit of continuous organizational learning,

improvement, and accountability; and (4) creating awareness and support for evaluation as a performance improvement strategy (King and Volkov, 2005). Process use and ECB may well be a marriage made in heaven.

Patton explicated the concept of process use—purposeful application of the evaluation process to teach evaluative inquiry—in the third edition of *Utilization-Focused Evaluation* (Patton, 1997), adding a separate chapter to distinguish use of the evaluation process from use of its findings. The idea was not entirely new. Almost a quarter century earlier, Merwin (1983) discussed the influence of both the process and the results of evaluations, and other writing (notably Rippey, 1973; King, 1988) discussed the effects of the evaluation process implicitly. But Patton's discussion of the specific outcomes of process use (for example, shared understanding or self-determination) focused attention on the potential benefits to people experiencing, or in some cases surviving, evaluation activities. Several years later, in a discussion of empowerment evaluation, Fetterman (2003) wrote: "Process use becomes a tool with which program staff members and participants build capacity. They internalize the logic of evaluation by conducting evaluation on a daily basis. As they use evaluation it becomes a part of the normal planning and management of the program, which is a means of institutionalizing evaluation" (p. 49).

Cousins, Goh, Clark, and Lee (2004) similarly connected process use with ECB, noting that process use is one mechanism through which evaluators can actively help organizations build evaluation capacity. They labeled process use ". . . a more indirect mode of evaluative inquiry leading to the development of evaluation capacity" (p. 106), noting that "in theory, if evaluation becomes integrated into the ongoing activities within an organization, it may become a learning system that fosters the development of shared values and understanding among organization members" (p. 107). Their review of empirical studies of both ECB and evaluation use identified connections between capacity building and use of evaluation with a "culture of evaluative inquiry or organizational readiness for evaluation" (p. 124).

As a concept, ECB is broad, much like utilization-focused evaluation. Like UFE, it is an overarching meta-approach that an evaluator can use with clients regardless of how a study is conducted; that is, it is distinct from specific roles or evaluative approaches. The ECB continuum (King and Stevahn, 2002, p. 8) highlights a number of possibilities for ECB in organizations. At one extreme, evaluators make no attempt to build capacity; they conduct a study as a one-time event, although by participating in the process—one example of process use—people may inadvertently learn evaluation skills. At the other extreme, an organization has purposefully built its evaluation capacity and engages in ongoing evaluative inquiry as a way of life—that is, as part of how it does business. King (1998), only somewhat tongue in cheek, calls this form of evaluative inquiry free-range evaluation. The concept of free-range evaluation captures the ultimate outcome of ECB: evaluative thinking that lives unfettered in an organization. It is "a process that is best done slowly and long-term" (King, 1998, p. 691). It is made stronger by freely moving among people, programs, and special projects, taking sustenance from its natural surroundings. Its vulnerability is also a strength: If it survives the challenges it confronts, it becomes stronger. In recent years, it has become the ultimate goal, the dependent variable, of my evaluation practice.

Between these extremes on the ECB continuum is the topic this chapter addresses: evaluators' active attempt to build evaluation capacity in a client's organization and intentional structuring of the evaluation process to do so. In framing ECB, it is important to distinguish between process use and process influence. The use literature, in recent years, has distinguished between evaluation use, which is direct, and influence, which is indirect (Kirkhart, 2000). This distinction matters in structuring process use for ECB. In this context, intentionality matters as well; someone must actively want to use the evaluation process to build capacity. As Preskill, Zuckerman, and Matthews (2003) write: "Perhaps our most important finding, though terribly obvious in hindsight, is that process use should be intentional. That is, if evaluators and organizations want people to learn from an evaluation's process, then certain conditions and processes need to be developed and supported from the evaluation's very beginning" (p. 438).

But, having made the decision to try, how can an evaluator engage people in activities that build evaluation capacity? The chapter presents specific suggestions for intentional process use and possible indicators, and it then offers brief examples—first positive, then negative—of organizations where staff and administrators purposefully set about building their internal capacity to think evaluatively.

Planning Intentional Process Use

To my mind, evaluation experiences should be educative; that is, the people who participate actively in an evaluation (often the primary intended users, to use Patton's term, but in some cases, many more individuals) should learn something as a result. This time-honored notion of the evaluator as teacher (Cronbach and others, 1980) suggests the four commonplaces of evaluative learning. Adapting Schwab's commonplaces (1969), the organizational milieu is the setting where evaluative learning occurs; the users/clients function as students or learners, the evaluator as teacher; and the evaluation process and its findings become the curriculum. In this view, evaluators can apply an understanding of the commonplaces to plan intentionally for ECB-oriented process use. This practice fits squarely in the realm of developmental evaluation, defined as "evaluation processes, including asking evaluative questions and applying evaluation logic, to support program, product, staff and/or organizational development" (Patton, 2007, p. 10). Patton continues: "The evaluator is part of a team whose members collaborate to conceptualize, design and test new approaches in a long-term, on-going process of continuous improvement, adaptation and intentional change" (p. 10). One way to do that is to bring process use to bear on the challenge of building evaluation capacity, a form of practice that some label distinct from program evaluation (Compton, Glover-Kudon, Smith, and Avery, 2002).

First, a caveat: Because the evaluator is taking an instructional role, there are no guarantees of success. As the teacher in the room next to mine once lamented at the end of sixth period, "I taught a great class today, but those students didn't learn a darn thing!" Some would argue that my colleague was wrong; it was not a great class, by definition, if students learned nothing. But the point is this: We evaluators may do everything we know to teach our intended users, but we cannot require anyone to *do* anything—the ongoing lament of a staff (as opposed to the line) relationship. My continuing hope is that by working with people who get evaluation for an extended period of time and by applying what we know about organizational change, we can establish procedures and structures that support free-range evaluation regardless of resource challenges or staff turnover, the Achilles heel of utilization-focused evaluation (Patton, 1997). In other words, not only will we lead the horse to water, but we help make the water cool and tantalizing and the horse's throat truly parched.

What follows are suggestions for using process use within the four ECB commonplaces—organizational context, evaluation champions, the evaluator/facilitator, and ECB infrastructure and process—that, taken together, may foster commitment to building an organization's ongoing evaluation capacity.

1. *Assess the organizational context to determine whether or not evaluation capacity building is viable.* Several of the situational analysis competencies from the "essential competencies for program evaluators" (Stevahn, King, Ghere, and Minnema, 2005) identify what to assess—for example, political considerations relevant to the evaluation and issues of potential evaluation use and of organizational change. Just as a cactus would fare poorly in a tropical rainforest, ECB is highly context sensitive. An initial step in intentional process use for ECB, then, is to assess both external and internal organizational contexts. Regardless of the content of our work in this new millennium, we live in an era of accountability, and it is first important to understand the evaluative pressures coming from the external environment. They include explicit mandates and accountability demands such as those required by legislation (for example, standardized testing at certain grade levels) or by funders' explicit reporting requirements (for example, client learning as a direct result of participation in a specific program), whether or not this is psychometrically or practically feasible. A second, more positive feature to assess in the external environment is the extent to which there is potential support for change (King and Volkov, 2005), perhaps through special funding to develop a certain kind of program or a funder who would be willing to collaborate with people on an innovative and improved evaluation process.

The internal organizational context also requires preliminary assessment, whether formal or informal. Applying a conceptual framework of evaluative inquiry (Cousins, Goh, Clark, and Lee, 2004) as an organizational learning system, one must first examine organizational readiness for building evaluation capacity, which includes assessing both existing organizational learning capacity and existing evaluation capacity. Process use has certain preconditions. Management support for using the evaluation process to learn is critical (Preskill, Zuckerman, and Matthews, 2003; King and Volkov, 2005). At a minimum, senior management must agree not to interfere with evaluation activities; better yet if they are willing to use their positional clout to encourage involvement and model support for the process. Preskill, Zuckerman, and Matthews (2003) identify other organizational characteristics to attend to, among them the degree of organizational stability, support for previous evaluation work, and the location and ownership of the evaluation function. King and Volkov (2005) suggest similar characteristics for examination, including determining if the internal environment is supportive of change, if there is broad-based interest in, and demand for, evaluation information, and the likely sources of support for evaluation in the organization. In addition, it is helpful to know early on the extent to which people who will participate in capacity-building activities have sufficient input into organizational decision making. Better to know sooner, not later, if the people engaged in the ECB process are unable to use evaluative information owing to existing power structures in the organization. Cousins and colleagues (2004) also add affective considerations, including people's willingness to generate new knowledge and question basic organizational assumptions as well as their inclination to use external information.

2. *Identify and support evaluation champions who will nurture evaluative thinking in themselves and others.* Process use requires engaged people—evaluation champions—which means that Patton's personal factor—the "presence of an identifiable individual or group of people who personally care about the evaluation and the findings it generates" (1997, p. 44)—must be alive, well, and living in the process use process. This commonplace highlights the need to quickly determine people's interest in, and commitment to, evaluation. In practice, it means two things. First, you must identify individuals who understand or intuitively get evaluation, that is, people who are willing to spend time with you discussing options, thinking about how to involve others, and eventually making sense of data. These may be your clients or those holding positional authority, but not necessarily. In every organization I have worked with, I have met people who simply enjoy the evaluation process, either because they understand it intuitively and are interested in learning more or because they have studied it somewhere, often in a degree program in the guise of a research methods course. One manager I know jokingly referred to herself as an "evaluation nerd" and then located others willing to admit publicly to that label.

NEW DIRECTIONS FOR EVALUATION • DOI: 10.1002/ev

Using the evaluation champions you have identified, a second action is to create an advisory group to manage and monitor the capacity-building process. In their exploratory study of successful evaluation advisory groups, Preskill, Zuckerman, and Matthews (2003) identified seven distinguishing attributes. Three of them—interest in the evaluation process, motivation to participate, and previous evaluation training and education—characterize evaluation champions. The remaining four—experience with the program; previous evaluation experience; role understanding; and position, rank, and experience—identify other variables appropriate for representation on the advisory group. My ongoing practice suggests the importance of purposefully including four kinds of members on an ECB advisory group (King, 2005):

1. The evaluation champions who will supply ongoing commitment, enthusiasm, and technical know-how.
2. Highly respected staff who know the organization's people and culture well. These individuals are typically top-notch practitioners, skilled at keeping a thumb on the organizational pulse and reading between the lines of others' comments. Others often seek them out.
3. Competent people who can get tasks done, regardless of the challenges faced. Although they may be new to evaluation, these folks are thorough and thoughtful, and you can count on them to deliver.
4. At least one person with a sense of humor and the ability to keep the capacity-building process in historical context—that is, to have an eye on the big picture this change seeks.

Three questions come to mind when I am charged with creating an advisory group. First, how large a group is large enough? As is often the case in evaluation practice, the answer is, "It depends." A small organization may need only three or four people on its advisory committee, especially if individuals represent two or more of the four categories. In a large organization, it may be helpful to structure two groups: (1) a small evaluation steering committee that actively manages the ECB process, and (2) a larger representative group that meets regularly (for example, monthly) to work on collective tasks such as instrumentation, data analysis and interpretation, and recommendation development. Second, should you include naysayers in this group? Again, it depends. If someone's negativity will block any possible progress, it seems counterintuitive to bring him or her into the inner circle. If, on the other hand, the person is open-minded enough to learn from the process and can represent potential constraints in the system, it may be worth including him or her. Third, should the advisory committee include clients, participants, or other end users? If process use is a class, then your advisory group needs to include everyone you hope to educate. If your intention is to train organizational staff to think evaluatively and reduce the strain on the evaluation budget, then those are the people to include on the advisory committee. If, by contrast, your intention is to teach community members through the evaluation process about how an organization is meeting their needs and the needs of the broader community, then they must be at the advisory committee table. The centrality of the long-term role of evaluation champions cannot be overstated. People, evaluators included, come and go. If evaluation is to survive in an organization, you must routinely create and sustain new supporters.

3. *Become purposeful about the evaluator's role as the facilitator of process use.* As noted earlier, the role of the evaluator in fostering process use requires intentionality and careful attention to capacity-building activities. An exploratory study identified facilitation of the evaluation process as one category of variables that affect process use (Preskill, Zuckerman, and Matthews, 2003): "If the facilitator treats individuals with respect, provides opportunities to engage in genuine dialogue and reflection, ensures that all voices are heard (no one feels silenced or marginalized), comes across as open-minded and trustworthy, and is not overly controlling, then it is likely that the group's learning will be greater" (p. 430).

Process use, then, is not for the faint of heart. Even though everyone else can get annoyed and visibly express frustration and angst, the evaluator must maintain a cheery calm in the face of every challenge. After hearing a damaging statement likely to threaten an evaluation I am conducting, I often say out loud, "Thank you for sharing that perspective; it is important to understand negative positions if we are to move forward." I am *thinking* something quite different, but this is not for the group to know. Feelings aside, I am sincere in noting the importance of having negative issues raised publicly if ECB is to be viable. The immediate question is how to resolve the expressed conflict quickly and in a way that supports the ongoing capacity-building process.

Several activities are required to facilitate process use: negotiating with key stakeholders before the evaluation begins, communicating effectively throughout the evaluation process, managing project details thoughtfully, and structuring constructive interpersonal interactions. The ability to identify the teachable moment—that instance during the process when participants can learn specific evaluation skills—is paramount. When your advisory committee reviews a data set that is bimodal and declares that because the two sides balance each other respondents are basically neutral, you face a teachable moment. Or when one of your key evaluation champions says that in a program that serves 50 percent students of color their parents just will not respond to a survey and so the evaluation should accept the fact there will be no data from them, you face a teachable moment. Identifying and responding to these moments requires a high level of interpersonal competence and several skill areas, including negotiation, conflict resolution, team building, group facilitation, and cross-cultural competence. Evaluators knowledgeable in the technical areas of qualitative and quantitative methods may feel stretched since evaluation training programs are unlikely to focus on such skills; however, resources exist for those interested in learning how to work effectively with groups (for example, Preskill and Russ-Eft, 2005; Stevahn and King, 2005; and formal facilitation trainings).

4. *Work with evaluation champions to construct an evaluation process and structures to support continuing evaluative thinking in the organization.* This is the fourth commonplace, the "curriculum" you will use with your partners to build evaluation capacity. What does this mean? Although one *New Directions* chapter cannot detail every likely activity, Volkov and King's ECB checklist (2006) identifies potential structures, including the need to make evaluation resources available over time. Let me highlight three activities that have proved useful in my practice. First, evaluators should work with key people in the organization to develop an "appropriate conception of and a tailored strategy for evaluation in organizational policies and procedures" (Volkov and King, 2006, p. 1) along with a purposeful, written capacity-building plan that explicitly frames the evaluation process to teach people evaluation skills and positive attitudes. It is not enough to discuss such a plan; written documents (an ECB plan, procedure manuals, policy statements) are important. Program evaluation intentions are often good but swept away in the stream of other demands. People can return to ECB documents after a period of time and note progress made—or the lack thereof. Revising the plan in light of organizational realities is always an option.

Second, evaluators can use various kinds of studies to model evaluative processes. The parallel with the balanced literacy movement, in which teachers teach children to read through diverse activities ranging from the teacher reading aloud to a group to students' independent work, is both striking and instructive. King and Stevahn's interactive continuum (2002) details the several roles an evaluator can play. At one extreme, in consultation with a client an evaluator can be completely in charge of designing and implementing a study; at the other, staff or participants can plan and conduct their own study in consultation with an evaluation coach. Midrange are various collaborative options that divide planning and implementation responsibilities according to the situation. An evaluator interested in fostering process use can take advantage of these roles to model and teach evaluation. So, for example, an evaluator-directed study can model how to effectively hire and use an outside evaluator when accountability demands a credible external evaluation. In a collaborative study, an evaluator can explicitly teach staff specific skills (sampling, how to conduct focus groups, survey item development), modeling as necessary to reinforce behaviors. With the support of an active coach, a staff-directed study can challenge individuals to walk the evaluation walk, knowing the coach will ensure a high-quality effort. The point is to use all aspects of an evaluation process—whatever it looks like—to teach people the evaluation process.

Third, it falls to the evaluator to help identify or create an organizational infrastructure to support the evaluation process over time, which is often challenging given our position within the organization, whether internal or external. I pay critical attention to people's purposeful socialization into the organization's evaluation process. Having a written plan and the commitment of leadership to use the evaluation process to teach staff or participants is all well and good, but if there is even a 20 percent turnover each year, then the capacity building process can quickly stall. Newcomers will not remember the magic moments when the advisory committee finished the agency's logic models or when program staff presented the results of an evaluation at a professional conference. They may well bring negative memories of evaluation long since past.

So, ideally, new staff are first handed a policy and procedures manual that details the *who, what, where,* and *when* of evaluation processes and then attend a personal training session that, in reviewing the manual collectively, explicates the *why* and *how.* Leadership must explicitly support this socialization so new hires understand that program evaluation is part of the organization's core operations, not an add-on or afterthought, but simply the way business is done. This helps to develop and sustain a cross-program network that reinforces evaluative thinking and that, in my experience, people enjoy. Such work builds on Forss, Rebien, and Carlsson's notion (2002) of developing professional networks and boosting morale as two types of process use.

Another of the types of process use that Forss and colleagues describe—learning to learn—is also vital. Peer learning structures specific to program evaluation (Volkov and King, 2006) create a place and time for interaction around evaluation information and reflection on the process. The advisory group may be one such structure, but it involves a relatively small number of people. The key question is how to engage multiple people in continuing discussions related to evaluative thinking so that many learn from ongoing activities. It means systematically and purposefully applying the experiential learning cycle—that is, planning an evaluation activity, doing it and collecting information about it, and then reflecting on what happened as one plans next steps. If possible, every member of the organization needs to understand that evaluation is a part of his or her job description, and there is a structure in place to support people in learning about what this means.

To summarize, lesson planning by applying the ECB commonplaces can give evaluators strategies for purposefully structuring process use. The first step is to assess the organizational context to determine whether or not ECB is even possible. The second is to identify and support evaluation champions who are willing to learn. Third, become purposeful about the evaluator's role as process use instructor. This is different from a singular focus on conducting program evaluations. The final step is to work in concert with the evaluation champions you have identified or are creating to establish structures and processes that nurture evaluative thinking over time. Given the complexity of even a small organization, there are no guarantees of success, but ongoing reflection can help people understand both progress and challenges.

Variables to Consider When Intentionally Using Process Use for ECB

Identifying variables affecting process use may support evaluators interested in building evaluation capacity. Stufflebeam's classic CIPP model emphasizes four aspects of program evaluation: context, input, process, and product, categories for possible process use variables (see Table 3.1). Applying them to ECB as a "program" suggests specific variables of interest. The content in Table 3.1 was initially developed from five process use sources: (1) the five categories of variables that "appear to affect process use" (Preskill, Zuckerman, and Matthews, 2003, p. 430); (2) Patton's primary uses of evaluation logic and processes, that is, the "impact of the evaluation [that] comes from application of evaluation thinking and engaging in evaluation processes (in contrast to impacts that come from using specific findings)" (1997, p. 111); (3) the five types of process use discussed in Forss, Rebien, and Carlsson (2002); (4) the literature review of Cousins, Goh, Clark, and Lee (2004); and (5) the Volkov and King (2005) ECB framework.

As discussed earlier, purposeful development of evaluation capacity through process use requires attention to organizational context, both outside and within. Many settings simply do not support these efforts. The input variables constitute a general checklist for evaluators prior to beginning an ECB project. Not surprisingly, the process variables are key to the process. In my opinion, it is easier to begin ECB than to sustain it over time, and monitoring these seven process variables may point to areas or activities that need bolstering. The product or outcome variables may be more important from an organizational perspective, and the pressing need for empirical research to document these outcomes is clear.

Brief Examples of Process Use for ECB

An old saying reminds us that Rome was not built in a day. The same is true of evaluation capacity when process use is the means to that end. As is the case with the practice of program evaluation, it is far easier to *write* about using process use to build evaluation capacity than to do it, or even more importantly to sustain it. What follows are two positive examples and four less-than-positive examples documenting the challenges an evaluator may face in seeking to take advantage of the evaluation process for purposes beyond an immediate evaluation study.

From 1999 to 2001, full-time and continuing on a part-time collaborative basis since then, I have worked with a large school district to build its evaluation capacity. Process use has been critical to this effort. When I was the full-time internal evaluator, we purposefully conducted numerous

Table 3.1. Possible Variables to Consider in Using Process Use to Build Evaluation Capacity

CIPP Components	What to Look at
Context (to define the institutional context, identify target population, diagnose problems, etc.)	*External context*: • External mandates and accountability requirements • Evidence of external support for change *Internal context*: • Management support • Broad-based interest in, and demand for, evaluation information • Commitment to use information • Willingness to generate new information • Willingness to question basic organizational assumptions
Input (to identify and assess system capabilities, program strategies, budgets, schedules, etc.)	• A purposeful evaluation capacity building (ECB) plan • Identifiable evaluation champions (including managers) • An established evaluation advisory group • Peer learning structures specific to evaluation • Infrastructure to support the evaluation process • Access to evaluation resources • Sufficient input into decision making
Process (to identify implementation issues, improvement, record processes, etc.)	• Systematic use of the organization's ECB plan • A viable evaluation advisory group • Incentives for participation in evaluation activities • Purposeful socialization into the evaluation process • Active facilitation of, and reflection on, evaluation processes • Documentation of existing evaluation resources • Ongoing and high-quality communication about evaluation
Product (to collect outcome data and interpret their merit and worth, etc.)	• Creation or enhancement of shared understandings • Increased staff or participant engagement and ownership • Support or reinforcement of program interventions • Program or organizational development • Increased networking (within the organization and without) • Increased morale • Increased organizational capacity to learn

Source: Descriptions of CIPP objectives from Fitzpatrick, Sanders, and Worthen (2004, p. 91).

types of study to teach people about program evaluation. One implementation study of the state's graduation standards was evaluator-directed, but with input from and reflection by a sizeable advisory group. Two other large evaluations—one on the special education department and one on implementation of the middle school concept—were more explicitly collaborative. In each case, I managed a small advisory group that actively prepared materials and activities for a larger study team, which in the case of special education was a team of more than fifty people. For the special education study, the district also hired two external evaluators to provide additional professional expertise; for the middle school study, I worked solo. Among other things, central office staff learned how to construct survey items, how to conduct focus groups, and how to analyze data—skills they report they continue to use. As an outsider, I am currently coaching district staff who are now using this structure to study the program for English language learners. Reflection on what is being learned about how to sustain program evaluation in a test-centric educational system is ongoing.

Process use is also part of capacity building for a well-established social service agency in West St. Paul, Minnesota. At Neighborhood House, a half-time evaluator's salary is supported by a small mandated percentage of every external grant. All staff—everyone—attends at least one half-day evaluation training session each year, along with other training opportunities, both local and national, as they are available. Within six months of their hiring, new staff are required to take Evaluation 101, a half-day introduction to the agency's evaluation process. Each program has its own logic model, which is studied and revised routinely. An evaluation advisory group (once proudly labeled the Evaluation Platoon)—which comprises the evaluator, the "computer guy," the assistant to the president, the vice president for programs, every program manager, and others as appropriate—meets monthly to monitor and oversee agencywide evaluation efforts and concerns. Numerous student and professional volunteers contribute to specific evaluation projects, and the agency board receives frequent communication about evaluation results. People learn evaluation by engaging in it and reflecting on it.

If positive examples point to possibilities, cautionary examples are also important. Here are four to suggest that discussion of building capacity internally, even when there are the intention and resources to do so, may be insufficient to create ongoing development through process use.

First, process use in an organization can be and often is easily hamstrung if no accessible or accurate database exists. This is a necessary part of the evaluation infrastructure and cannot be taken for granted. Early in my tenure at the school district, for example, I was pleased to learn that student outcome data (usually standardized test scores) existed, but unfortunately not in my department. I could send a request asking for the scores to a hard-working clerk who already had a full-time job, and my request went on her "when I get to it" pile. I could also ask my boss to request the data, but to do so regularly would not have set well within the administrative hierarchy. Here, clearly, was a problem to be solved. Technological advances and a commitment for more immediate access to data have resolved this. More recently, lack of a reliable database has been the bane of internal evaluators at several large Twin Cities (Minnesota) social service agencies, including Neighborhood House. It is extremely difficult to use an evaluation process instructionally if you lack confidence in your data or your ability to produce data accurately when needed. The Alliance of Connected Communities, a collaboration of more than twenty Twin Cities community centers, is working to address this issue across its member agencies.

Second, in one case, a large informal educational institution solved the ECB "problem" by hiring two internal evaluators and then paying consultants by the project to conduct needed studies. But by compartmentalizing the work—that is, as the work became the domain and responsibility of the two full-time evaluators and the occasional part-time hires, other staff no longer need to engage in collective discussion of overarching concerns and procedures. Yes, there was increased capacity to conduct evaluations, but only minimal process use.

Third, process use changes character in large, multisite program evaluations, such as those sponsored by state and federal agencies (see, for example, Lawrenz, Huffman, and McGinnis, in this volume). One tack that certain projects have taken is to encourage evaluators from around the country to participate voluntarily in cross-site conversations, both electronically and, when possible, in person. The assumption seems to be that individual practitioners use the process to improve their evaluations while simultaneously increasing their evaluative skills; in addition, the cross-site sponsor compiles the collective learnings. It strikes me, however, that the voluntary nature of the participation and the logistics of long-distance communication make this form of process use particularly difficult.

Fourth, a cautionary illustration comes from a private foundation, which was studied because the organization purportedly was engaged in ECB and had extensive resources to do so (Volkov, 2007). In this case, money was literally no object, and a number of factors (notably, pressure from the board of directors and support from foundation leadership) supported the process. Nevertheless, the combination of urgent competing priorities, lack of buy-in on the part of many staff, and insufficient consistency around evaluation resulted over two years in an end to the capacity-building effort.

As these examples suggest, even at its best, sustaining process use to build evaluation capacity over time can challenge the skills of the most experienced facilitator.

A colleague of mine who studies school change uses a video clip of a team of construction workers building a plane while it is flying, bringing an often-cited image to life. The scenes inevitably draw laughter—as the flight attendant pours coffee, the stream of hot liquid pours onto a person in the next row, and the open sky visible through the lattice work of the plane's body is a steady reminder that everyone is thirty thousand feet above the earth. At the end of the clip, the construction workers parachute off; the crew and passengers remain on board. The parallels with process use are clear. ECB through process use requires that people who are flying the evaluation plane build evaluation capacity while they are in the air. The organization needs to get the evaluation completed, and learning from the process as it happens may threaten people's ability to get this critical job done. The builder-evaluator pays attention to creating opportunities for learning, but not everyone wants to learn or feels comfortable with the topic. Pilot and crew must commit to dual tasks. What is often heartening in my experience is the commitment that many people are willing to make—those who see the potential that program evaluation holds for their organization and can imagine the completed plane taking them to new heights.

References

Compton, D. W., Glover-Kudon, R., Smith, I. E., and Avery, M. E. "Ongoing Capacity Building in the American Cancer Society." In D. W. Compton, M. Baizerman, and S. Hueftle Stockdill (eds.), *The Art, Craft, and Science of Evaluation Capacity Building. New Directions for Evaluation,* no. 93. San Francisco: Jossey-Bass, 2002.

Cronbach, L. J., and others. *Toward Reform of Program Evaluation.* San Francisco: Jossey-Bass, 1980.

Cousins, J. B., Goh, S. C., Clark, S., and Lee, L. E. "Integrating Evaluative Inquiry into the Organizational Culture: A Review and Synthesis of the Knowledge Base." *Canadian Journal of Program Evaluation,* 2004, *19*(2), 99–141.

Fetterman, D. "Fetterman-House: A Process Use Distinction and a Theory." In C. A. Christie (ed.), *The Practice-Theory Relationship in Evaluation. New Directions for Evaluation,* no. 97. San Francisco: Jossey-Bass, 2003.

Forss, K., Rebien, C. C., and Carlsson, J. "Process Use in Evaluation." *Evaluation,* 2002, *8*(1), 29–45.

King, J. A. "Research on Evaluation Use and Its Implications for the Improvement of Evaluation Research and Practice." *Studies in Educational Evaluation,* 1988, *4*, 285–299.

King, J. A. "Becoming Pragmatist." Invited keynote at the annual meeting of the Australasian Evaluation Society, Melbourne, Australia, Oct. 1998.

King, J. A. "A Proposal to Build Evaluation Capacity at the Bunche-Da Vinci Learning Partnership Academy." In M. C. Alkin and C. A. Christie (eds.), *Theorists' Models in Action. New Directions for Evaluation,* no. 106. San Francisco: Jossey-Bass, 2005.

King, J. A., and Pechman, E. M. "Pinning a Wave to the Shore: Conceptualizing School Evaluation Use." *Educational Evaluation and Policy Analysis,* 1984, *6*(3), 241–251.

King, J. A., and Stevahn, L. "Three Frameworks for Considering Evaluator Role." In K. E. Ryan and T. A. Schwandt (eds.), *Exploring Evaluator Role and Identity.* Greenwich, Conn.: Information Age, 2002.

King, J. A., and Volkov, B. "A Grounded Framework for Evaluation Capacity Building." Paper presented at the annual meeting of the American Evaluation Association, Atlanta, Ga. Nov., 2004.

King, J. A., and Volkov, B. "A Framework for Building Evaluation Capacity Based on the Experiences of Three Organizations." *CURA* [Center for Urban and Regional Affairs] *Reporter,* 2005, *35*(3) 10–16.

Kirkhart, K. "Reconceptualizing Evaluation Use: An Integrated Theory of Influence." In V. Caracelli (ed.), *The Expanding Scope of Evaluation Use. New Directions for Evaluation,* no. 88. San Francisco: Jossey-Bass, 2000.

Merwin, J. C. "Dimensions of Evaluation Impact." *The Utilization of Evaluation: Proceedings of the Minnesota Evaluation Conference,* Minneapolis, Minn. May 1983.

Patton, M. Q. *Utilization-Focused Evaluation* (3rd ed.). Thousand Oaks, Calif.: Sage, 1997.

Patton, M. Q. "Developmental Evaluation." Handout from a workshop conducted at the 2007 Minnesota Evaluation Studies Institute, Bloomington, Minn., March 2007.

Preskill, H., and Russ-Eft, D. *Building Evaluation Capacity: Seventy-Two Activities for Teaching and Training.* Thousand Oaks, Calif.: Sage, 2005.

Preskill, H., Zuckerman, B., and Matthews, B. "An Exploratory Study of Process Use: Findings and Implications for Future Research." *American Journal of Evaluation,* 2003, 24(4), 423–442.

Rippey, R. M. (ed.). *Studies in Transactional Evaluation.* Berkeley, Calif.: McCutchan, 1973.

Schwab, J. "The Practical: A Language for Curriculum." *School Review,* 1969, 78(1), 1–23.

Stevahn, L., and King, J. A. "Managing Conflict Constructively in Program Evaluation." *Evaluation,* 2005, 11(4), 415–427.

Stevahn, L., King, J. A., Ghere, G. S., and Minnema, J. "Establishing Essential Competencies for Program Evaluators." *American Journal of Evaluation,* 2005, 26, 49–51.

Volkov, B. "Toward Enhanced Quality, Learning, and Continuous Improvement in Organizations: A Case Study of Evaluation Capacity Building in the Northwest Area Foundation." Unpublished doctoral dissertation, University of Minnesota, 2007.

Volkov, B., and King, J. A. "A Checklist for Building Evaluation Capacity." Paper presented at the joint meeting of the American Evaluation Association and the Canadian Evaluation Society, Toronto, Nov., 2005.

Volkov, B., and King, J. A. "Evaluation Capacity Building Checklist." Unpublished manuscript, University of Minnesota, 2006.

JEAN A. KING *teaches evaluation studies in the Department of Educational Policy and Administration at the University of Minnesota.*

NEW DIRECTIONS FOR EVALUATION • DOI: 10.1002/ev

*This chapter presents a case report of Canada's
International Development Research Centre's success in
revamping its project reporting system. The new process
has transformed the organization's culture and deepened
evaluative capacity, thus promoting accountability for
the management of public funds and the ability to learn
and improve.*

Infusing Evaluative Thinking as Process Use: The Case of the International Development Research Centre (IDRC)

Fred Carden, Sarah Earl

Introduction

Until the recent introduction of a dynamic interview-based process, the International Development Research Centre (IDRC; http://www.idrc.ca), a Canadian development research funding agency, faced a challenge: project completion reports (PCRs) were not being completed in a timely and quality manner. This is a common problem many organizations face in completing evaluation reports. For more than a decade, a PCR was a static document that IDRC project managers were required to prepare at the end of a research project, to capture its results and lessons. We had a sophisticated evaluation and performance management system at IDRC, but we had to face the reality that at the most fundamental level, many project managers were not completing the required end-of-project reports. This was noted during the course of a routine examination of Centre management practices by the auditor general of Canada.[1] This failure was not acceptable to anyone in the organization; we strive to ensure that evaluation is a useful process that develops the evaluation capacity of everyone engaged in it. This attitude is the foundation of the deep culture of evaluation and evaluative thinking the Evaluation Unit has built at IDRC.[2]

NEW DIRECTIONS FOR EVALUATION, no. 116, Winter 2007 © Wiley Periodicals, Inc.
Published online in Wiley InterScience (www.interscience.wiley.com) • DOI: 10.1002/ev.243

This chapter describes IDRC's struggle to make a mundane paperwork exercise—writing project completion reports—contribute to organizational learning and accountability. It describes how the center successfully transformed a bureaucratic paper system into a dynamic interviewing and learning process, renamed rolling Project Completion Reports (rPCRs), in just eighteen months. When we began in November 2003, we had a backlog of almost 580 outstanding reports. By December 2004, the backlog was cleared to zero. To date, there has been no significant backsliding. Project managers are completing the reports on time, the organization is analyzing and using the data they provide regularly, and staff members' ability to engage in evaluative thinking has grown significantly. Their interviewing skills, pattern recognition capabilities, and data interpretation skills have all deepened as a result.

In tackling this issue, we did not consciously use the language of "process use"; nor did we approach this exercise theoretically. We had a problem to fix. Over a year and a half, we developed and tested a solution that has now been operating for more than two years. Our case relates to this volume on process use because it demonstrates that the way to fix our "paperwork problem" was to focus on the process, bringing it more in line with our organizational approach to evaluation. This meant strengthening evaluation capacity and evaluative thinking through the process of completing and analyzing the findings of rPCRs. Even though the rPCR is not strictly an evaluation, it is an evaluative process and part of the center's overall evaluation system. We hope that IDRC's experience will illuminate some of the opportunities and challenges around operationalizing process use in an organizational context.

IDRC and Evaluation at IDRC

IDRC is a Crown corporation. The Parliament of Canada created the center in 1970 to help developing countries use science and technology to find practical, long-term solutions to social, economic, and environmental problems. IDRC support is directed toward developing an indigenous research capacity to sustain policies and technologies that developing countries need to build healthier, more equitable, and more prosperous societies. In carrying out its central mission, *empowerment through knowledge,* IDRC finances applied research and provides expert advice for researchers in developing countries, while building local capacity for research and innovation.

IDRC recognizes the essential role that evaluation plays in managing research projects effectively and producing relevant results from the research process. The center's overall approach to evaluation prioritizes equally the use and adoption of evaluation findings obtained through application of rigorous methods and the development of evaluative thinking capacities through evaluation processes. In 1992, IDRC established a small unit to coordinate the center's evaluation efforts. The Evaluation Unit supports the

NEW DIRECTIONS FOR EVALUATION • DOI: 10.1002/ev

priorities of the center by promoting methodological development and processes of evaluative thinking that balance the opportunity to learn and the need for accountability.

IDRC's approach to evaluation is utilization-focused. The center does not advocate any particular evaluation model, method, or theory. By promoting the appropriate methodology for a particular use, the center acknowledges that no one methodology fits every situation. Rather, the primary users and uses of evaluation should guide the selection of the most appropriate focus, methodology, and approach.

The center's approach to evaluation focuses on encouraging a broad range of partners to participate in, and take ownership of, an evaluation. Social participation is a critical outcome of the evaluation process; the process contributes to better, more transparent governance. Through our work to strengthen evaluation capacity and enlarge the field of evaluation for development organizations, IDRC contributes not only to a more effective development research community, but also to evidenced-based decision making more broadly.

The Problem.   Since IDRC's founding in 1970, we have used projects to build research capacity and finance research activities. IDRC's program staff identifies good projects and project leaders. Once these projects are identified and their parameters agreed on, IDRC funds them for two to three years, with additional phases of support possible. The Archives of Canada permanently stores core documentation about the projects. This documentation includes project proposals, approval documents from the center, and final project completion reports that project managers prepare.

A key contributing factor to the ongoing problem with PCR completion was the significant changes in structure, staff, and resources in the 1990s. Even though the reports were always viewed as important, they had become a burden and by 2003 "PCR avoidance" was well established. A further contributing factor was that when the time came to write a report, the responsible project manager was involved in new work and new projects. These new activities often took precedence—not just for the project manager, but for administrators and organizational managers as well. Members of the Evaluation Unit were the primary users of the reports. The unit drew on them to identify issues to evaluate, look for cross-cutting trends, and identify projects for follow-up attention. The unit was concerned about the reports awaiting completion, of course, but also about the poor quality of some of the reports. As the primary user, the unit was seen as the owner of the reporting system.

In the past, when IDRC tried to fix the PCR problem, we attacked the backlog from several directions. We tried cajoling or obligating, with no success (management fix). We worked with program staff to redesign the questions (participation and design fix). We restructured the paper and online templates for completing the reports (technical fix). We hired summer staff to help project managers decrease the backlog (human resource fix). After every attempt, IDRC wrote off some of the reports, either because the project area was no longer relevant to current programming or because the project manager had left the center, and it was difficult to complete the reports only by reviewing files. Although this approach reduced the backlog temporarily, it inevitably returned, as IDRC approved more projects.

When the problem came to the attention of the auditor general of Canada, who reported on it in a special examination in 2003,[3] the resulting criticism served as an impetus for renewed effort to address the backlog. We started by reassessing the need for project completion reports. Were they useful? If so, what could the center do to change the process involved in producing them?

Led by the president, senior managers were unified in their commitment to the reports and viewed them as central to the process of accounting for expenditure of public funds. The center's challenge was to figure out how to change the process and organizational culture to bring our reporting up to date and prevent any backsliding.

Revamping the Process. It was clear that this was an organizationwide problem. The first step was to engage the Programs and Partnership Branch, the group responsible for financing and managing projects and reporting their results. The reports had to be reinstated as being integral to IDRC's philosophy of supporting development research.

To that end, the center created a PCR Working Group. A manager from the Evaluation Unit and another from Programs and Partnership cochaired the group. It included representatives from staff responsible for completing the reports; from the Evaluation Unit, which used them; and from the information technology team responsible for developing a storage and retrieval system. For eighteen months, the group met monthly over lunch to design a solution.

Through an internal action research project, the working group discovered that one of the core problems with the quality of the reports was that staff were asked to complete them at a point in a project's lifespan—the conclusion—when the project managers were learning the least and, as a result, were least engaged in the project. The project managers were most engaged and learned the most during the design phase of a project and in the early days of implementation. We built this knowledge into our redesigned process.

The working group identified some other problems. The reports were not easily accessible to those who wanted to use them. Because of changes in information systems as well as earlier attempts to change the project templates, PCRs had become increasingly difficult to find and read. To solve this aspect of the problem, we designed a new filing protocol, identified all the PCRs, and filed about fifteen hundred reports in an accessible database. We then trained staff on the filing protocol so they could store and find the reports.

We also discovered that the reports were essentially solitary endeavors, largely unread and unused. So we devised an interview format for preparing the reports. This immediately engaged at least two people in the process, who could then learn about the project. This restructuring of the format helped to create a broader discussion, particularly in the Programs and Partnership Branch, about the results the projects generated. Managers also received more detailed information about projects than they had garnered in the past. They could then use this knowledge in their own reports. This helped generate incentives for completing the reports.

After redesigning the report process, we asked staff responsible for writing them to test the new procedures. First, we trained them to improve their interviewing skills. We also assigned one member of the working group to each test group. The working group members helped staff with template questions, obtained immediate feedback concerning their reactions to the new system, and reported back to the entire working group. This approach allowed us to adjust the new process and our training methods before we presented them to senior managers. For example, we altered the wording, order, and content of the questions; decided on who was best placed to play the role of interviewer and at which stage; and developed a policy on how many projects would require all three stages of interviews and how many would require only the final stage.

Encouraging Buy-in

At each step along the way in developing this new reporting process, the PCR Working Group kept senior managers informed, to sustain their interest and solicit their support. As a result, once the working group presented the final proposal to the senior management committee, managers understood it, supported it, and approved it.

To further signal the need for senior managers to become involved and buy in to this new process, we departed from conventional procedure by preparing a formal resolution that called for IDRC's president to sign the proposal. This level of formality was unusual for management committee meetings. It sent the message that this change was not just one more attempt to reduce the backlog of reports, but was also introducing a truly transformative process that would change the culture of the organization.

The Solution: Rolling Project Completion Reports (rPCRs)

After wide consultation, IDRC introduced a more appropriate form of project evaluation, renamed the rolling Project Completion Report (rPCR). Under the old template, project managers prepared a single report at the end of a project. As the new name suggests, "rolling" reports result from interviews conducted at three stages of the project: after initial design, roughly at the project midpoint, and finally at the end.

Early in the life of a project, a junior staff member interviews the responsible project manager. He or she gathers data about project design, start-up lessons, and issues that require future attention. In the middle of a project, team leaders interview the project manager to capture lessons about implementation and interim outcomes, and to update work on major issues flagged in the first interview. After the end of a project, the project manager selects the most appropriate colleague or manager to interview him or her, identify results, and capture any pertinent lessons.

In training senior managers on interviewing in the rPCR process through practical application, one manager noted, "This is a centrally important element of my work" (IDRC, 2006b, p. 2). The interview training was conducted with all levels of staff who would be involved. In the evaluations of the interview trainings, staff commented on the value of interviews in making them think more carefully about their work. They also noted they would apply their new interviewing skills in other dimensions of their work (IDRC, 2005).

This process ensures that knowledge is shared broadly within IDRC. Individual project managers learn more because of the dynamic process, and others in the organization benefit from their knowledge as well. The result is a collective experience and accumulated knowledge. For example, in our Asia program on information and communication technologies for development (ICT4D), the findings from interviews on projects that worked with the government of Cambodia led the team to explore further their experiences supporting research through government departments.

The redesign was more than a technical adjustment; it was intended to change workplace culture. Rolling Project Completion Reports are part of a realistic, useful process designed to engage employees and managers; improve their effectiveness; generate, capture, and store information and knowledge at the project level; and fulfill accountability requirements.

In the follow-up review with staff that had been conducting rPCR interviews after one year, a staff member noted: "I think it is quite good to talk about issues. It also tends to refresh issues in your mind as you talk about them. The same time as you do the interview you start thinking about other issues and it is not the same as writing it down. This is a good process . . ." (Haylock, 2006, p. 5).

This is consistent with many of the comments by interviewees ("it makes you actually think about things"; Haylock, 2006, p. 5) on the evaluative thinking that went into completion of the rPCRs.

The core of the new system involves interactive, open-ended interviews about the goals, methods, results, and lessons from the projects that IDRC funds. Each interview is conducted with a set of standard questions. The reflective aspect of the exchange is a learning opportunity for both the interviewer and the interviewee. Because many participants are spread out in offices around the world, the conversations often take place over the telephone. The interview is directly typed into a computer and later edited for the written record.

Each interview has a unique purpose. The first interview aims to stimulate reflection that goes beyond what the funding appraisal considered.

Project managers are encouraged to imagine the additional learning that can take place during the life of the project. The second interview focuses on the content and progress of the project: what has gone well, what problems exist, and how the project team is working. The second interview also captures any practical lessons that can be applied to other projects. The third interview is critical for accountability. It concentrates on the project's relative success: Has the project achieved its objectives? What are the outputs and outcomes? Each interview is connected and builds on issues raised in the previous interview. This thematic connection allows the interviewees to deepen their understanding of the project and the lessons they can draw from it. The process is designed so that the interviewee's responses are entered in real time, with subsequent opportunities for the project manager to correct and append supporting documentation and cross-reference information sources.

IDRC is concerned with whether taxpayer dollars produced intended results and is also interested in processes, people, and contexts that contribute to change. By focusing on both results and processes, we demonstrate the outcomes of our development research, as well as capture a rich supply of knowledge and lessons we can apply in other situations. To further validate project results, we periodically triangulate the aggregate lessons that the interviews identify with the results of independent evaluation, expert opinion, and experiences that our partner organizations (often other project donors) identify. This allows the center to place more confidence in the significance and transferability of what we report.

For the rPCR process to be applicable to our organization, we amended some standard evaluation methods. For example, the interviewers are not neutral parties; they are active participants who are expected to learn during the interview. Nor are the interviews completely open-ended. The interviewer has a template to follow but may probe further on any issue he or she believes is relevant. Interviewers may even occasionally interject with their own opinion, although the interviewers have been encouraged to wait until the end of the interview to do that. We also compromised on the transcripts. To cut down on the workload involved, we do not capture them verbatim. The interviewer paraphrases the conversation, and it is then sent to the project manager for final approval.

Before we began the new process, we gave all of the interviewers, from junior program staff to senior managers, training on interview techniques. This was the first area of evaluation capacity development. The training addressed standard issues: how to probe effectively, how to ask questions while typing simultaneously, how to manage an interview subject who strays off-topic, and so on. We also looked at specific organizational challenges, such as how to switch from the managerial function of assessing employees' performance to the neutral role of nonjudgmental interviewer. We also looked at how to encourage colleagues to reflect deeply and discuss sensitive or political information, knowing that the transcripts of these interviews would be shared within the organization. Through the training, the interviewers became more fully committed to the rPCR process and began to understand the broad organizational knowledge the interviews seek to deliver. The interviewers also realized that they are integral to IDRC's ability, as an organization, to learn and grow because they determine what is captured in each transcript. This information, in turn, is the critical means by which knowledge is shared throughout the organization.

The Annual Learning Forum

Staff at all levels in IDRC use the knowledge that the rPCR process generates in daily programming. A formal part of the process is an Annual Learning Forum we created to disseminate knowledge throughout the organization. Like the interview process, the forum reflects what is primarily an oral culture at IDRC. It draws on the idea that conversation and reflection among colleagues can elicit tacit knowledge people have not yet shared.

In alternate years, the forum consists of a daylong staff event or a series of smaller, program-based team meetings at IDRC's Ottawa headquarters and regional offices.

The forum shares material the rPCR process produces and data from other evaluations among colleagues, regions, and program areas. Employing group facilitation techniques, we encourage a relaxed and engaging atmosphere. In 2005, the first forum discussed "The Public Policy Influence of Networks" and "Network Sustainability." In 2006, each program and regional office decided on its own topic. At the 2007 all-staff forum, the topic was "Strengthening Organizational Capacity."

In the evaluation of the Annual Learning Forum in 2007, one participant summed up the process use of the event: "Sharing with all staff about issues they are struggling with—noting that in a way they are my own issues. The collectivity in findings solutions was interesting" (IDRC, 2007, p. 2).

The center does not use the forum to plan or make decisions. Instead, we take time as a community to generate and share knowledge and experiences. The forum serves as a venue to discover what individuals and the group know, on some level, but have not yet shared. When colleagues compare their experiences, question one another, explore contexts, search for patterns, analyze differences, and debate concepts, this tacit knowledge surfaces. What comes to the fore is not always an abstract idea or a grand theory. Practical nuggets of information, such as tips, personal contacts, references to books and articles, and anecdotes are both valued and valuable in the search to discover what works and what does not work in support of development research.

In addition to asking "What have we accomplished?" the forum asks "Why?" and "How?" Colleagues analyze their experiences in order to make better informed, more nuanced decisions later. IDRC works in a complex global context where there are seldom easy answers. The forum challenges staff to do better, be innovative, and take risks while striving to improve the organization's overall performance. The forum instills an inquisitive and evaluative culture where imagination, rumination, creativity, and debate become hallmarks of the work environment.

Assessing the Impact. During a retreat in 2001, IDRC's Senior Management Committee (SMC) expanded the organization's evaluation commitment to include a framework for performance assessment at the overall corporate level. This involved systematic collection of performance data regarding IDRC's strategic goals and operating principles. To begin, senior managers identified those principles they expected would permeate all of the center's work in accomplishing our two overall strategic goals: (1) indigenous capacity building and (2) policy and technology influence. The managers committed the organization to monitor not just results against these two strategic goals but also the extent to which the center was employing its fundamental operating principles. One of these operating principles was evaluative thinking.

Senior management defined good corporate performance in evaluative thinking in this way: "The Centre supports evaluative thinking by staff and partner organizations in the effort to be clear and specific about the results being sought, the means used to achieve these results, and to assure the systematic use of evidence to demonstrate achievement for both learning and accountability purposes." Three characteristics of how this good performance is manifested in the organization are:

1. "Undertaking, using and reflecting on the outcomes that our evaluations of high-quality projects and programs generate, using that information to inform decisions about program and project design and implementation"
2. "Allocating time and resources to staff and partner organizations so they can enhance their monitoring and evaluation capacities"
3. "Setting clear corporate goals and operating principles, and using evaluation data and other performance information to inform the decisions and perspectives of senior managers and the Board of Governors" [IDRC, 2006a, p. 20].

By engaging in the process of completing and analyzing the findings of project reports, we have strengthened the evaluative thinking and evaluation capacity of the center, in keeping with our organizational definition of good performance. These improvements have occurred at the individual staff, management, and corporate levels. Deepening evaluative thinking has resulted in improved accountability concerning our management of public funds and more effective research for development projects and programs.

One example of the difference that the rPCR process has made concerns the increased comfort of senior managers in receiving and acting on performance data. Every six months, the Evaluation Unit reports the rPCR completion rate to IDRC's Senior Management Committee. This regular reporting is seen as essential to ensuring that the backlog of reports does not return. The biannual report includes the total project reports completed, those exempted, the number of late reports, the number of program staff with more than three late reports, and the names of senior managers with late reports. On receiving these figures, senior managers engage in a discussion around three questions:

1. Were the follow-up actions that were decided on at the last meeting carried out?
2. How does senior management interpret these new figures?
3. What actions need to be taken by senior management or by others in the organization?

This process is now routine and effective. Senior managers review the data, interpret their meaning in the context of the center's performance, and rectify any problems. The managers also look for ways to improve the process. To date, this has taken many forms: improving the searchability of the reports, revising job descriptions to include the tasks associated with the report process, and recognizing the work that went into implementing the system. In many ways, we have moved to an ideal example of senior management's use of performance data.

This was not the case, however, at the outset. Receiving the first report from the Evaluation Unit, senior managers reacted promptly but negatively. They were upset at being "ambushed" with a report that indicated project reports were late, that some staff members had more than three reports overdue, and that six senior managers were themselves late with the reports for their projects.

The center worked past this reaction quickly. We did so by defining what constitutes "normal" performance data on the report completion rate. For example, staff changes, project extensions, and errors in reporting mean there will always be some late project reports. There are also peaks and valleys in the completion rate. In some quarters, project appropriations and other deadlines dictate a lower report completion rate than at other times. Regular reporting on completion rate has allowed managers to monitor and improve implementation of the rPCR process.

As IDRC implemented the new project reporting process, we have made concrete changes to improve the operation and utility of rPCRs in the organization. The next challenge we face is to measure the difference this new process makes in our programming. Management has challenged the center to measure whether greater evaluative thinking through the rPCR process has improved IDRC's support of research for development.

If IDRC's approach were merely to furnish grants, it would be extremely difficult to measure the impact of evaluative thinking. However, IDRC's approach emphasizes providing technical assistance in substantive research, networking building, and capacity building. The center should be able to see project managers offering more refined and useful advice to project partners because of their reflection on their own experience and their access to other colleagues' learning. At a program level, we should also be able to see uptake of knowledge from other colleagues in the design of programs, the interventions used, the problem-solving skills of staff, and their willingness to engage in evaluation processes with partners, making us a better and more accountable organization.

Conclusion

Long disdained, rPCRs have now become a source of energy and enlightenment, and a manifestation of evaluative thinking infused into our organizational culture. The new process has helped IDRC strengthen the culture of reflection that increases our knowledge and accountability. In the end, we retain more of what we learn, and we function more efficiently and effectively in our support of research for development. Now that the reports are completed regularly, the center is integrating them into our evaluation system more effectively, and we can triangulate them with external evaluations, program reviews, and other sources of evaluative data.

Changing the way IDRC dealt with project completion reporting was neither simple nor smooth. We had to deal with two conflicting patterns in the organization. Though the workplace culture is primarily oral and so should have been accepting of the use of interviews as a way to gather data, project management is an individual skill. The interview process did not come naturally to everyone. It took time for people to grow comfortable with it, and to appreciate its benefits.

Other challenges remain. In an organization whose mental model is "innovation equals competency," we will need to modify the process and remain inventive in terms of how we do so, on an ongoing basis. One question is whether we will be able to involve our project partners in this evaluation process. For the time being, we have decided to keep the process as an internal tool, on the principle that we could not ask our partners to change until we ourselves have changed.

The new project reporting system is only one part of our overall evaluation system, which balances learning and accountability at the project, program, and corporate levels. The process works alongside a variety of evaluation and reporting mechanisms that we developed to meet specific organizational needs. As it is implemented, it will continue to evolve to meet changing conditions in the center. Part of what made our adoption of this new system work was that a series of factors came into play simultaneously:

- Ownership of the rPCR process shifted from the Evaluation Unit to the Programs and Partnership Branch.
- The working environment throughout the Canadian federal government shifted to increase its emphasis on accountability and reporting.
- The working group, with strong leadership from programs, operated effectively as a team and acted as ambassadors for the new approach.
- We built on organizational strengths, such as our oral culture.
- We were able, through the Annual Learning Forum, to demonstrate active and effective use of the findings the reports generated.

We present this case because we think it illustrates certain lessons that others may be able to use in designing evaluation for process use. One of the major lessons IDRC learned was that evaluation processes need to fit the culture and context of an organization. They must be geared toward specific uses. Another lesson is that learning processes take time in order to be rigorous and useful. There is a need to balance the desire to improve with ongoing work demands. Finding the right balance takes time and, once found, still needs to be periodically revisited because it will shift. We do not suggest that other organizations should adopt our process holus-bolus. But as an illustration of use of the evaluation process to foster evaluative thinking and develop evaluation capacity in an organization, we think that the rolling Project Completion Report process at IDRC has merit for the broader evaluation community.

Notes

1. International Development Research Centre Special Examination Report 27, Mar. 2003 (http://www.idrc.ca/en/ev-101968-201-1-DO_TOPIC.html).
2. Evaluative thinking shifts the view of evaluation from only the study of completed projects and program toward an analytical way of thinking that infuses and informs everything the center does. Evaluative thinking is being clear and specific about what results are sought and what means are used to achieve them. It ensures systematic use of evidence to report on progress and achievements. Thus information informs action and decision making.
3. "There is a major backlog in the preparation of project completion reports." International Development Research Centre Special Examination Report 27, Mar. 2003, p. 12 (http://www.idrc.ca/en/ev-101968-201-1-DO_TOPIC.html).

References

Haylock, L. "Working Paper: Review of 1 Year of IDRC Experience Implementing Stage 1 of the rPCR Process (August 2005-August 2006)." Ottawa: Evaluation Unit, IDRC, 2006.

International Development Research Centre. *Special Examination Report* (http://www.idrc.ca/en/ev-101968–201–1-D)_TOPIC.html), Mar. 27, 2003.

International Development Research Centre. *rPCR Interview Workshop: Training Evaluation Results*. Ottawa: IDRC, 2005.

International Development Research Centre. *Corporate Assessment Framework*. Ottawa: IDRC, 2006a.

International Development Research Centre. *rPCR Interview Workshop: Workshop Evaluation Results.* Ottawa: IDRC, 2006b.

International Development Research Centre. *Evaluation of ALF 2007,* Ottawa: IDRC, 2007.

FRED CARDEN *is director of evaluation at the International Development Research Centre (IDRC Canada) and coauthor of outcome mapping and several books and articles on organizational assessment.*

SARAH EARL *is senior program officer in the Evaluation Unit of IDRC Canada.*

NEW DIRECTIONS FOR EVALUATION • DOI: 10.1002/ev

5

This chapter describes the issues surrounding evaluation process use in a large, national, multilevel, multisite evaluation funded by the National Science Foundation. Two key questions that emerge from this chapter are to what extent a multilevel core evaluation can affect evaluation process use and what types of process use can be affected.

Multilevel Evaluation Process Use in Large-Scale Multisite Evaluation

Frances Lawrenz, Douglas Huffman, J. Randy McGinnis

In this chapter, we examine evaluation process use in a large multilevel, multisite core evaluation. According to Patton, evaluation process use is defined as "individual changes in thinking and behavior, and program or organizational changes in procedures and culture, that occur among those involved in the evaluation as a result of the learning that occurs during the evaluation process" (1997, p. 90). Patton (1998) suggests that process use may include learning to learn, qualitative insights, and goal displacement. Forss, Rebien, and Carlsson (2002) suggest four primary kinds of process use: enhancing shared understandings; supporting and reinforcing the program through intervention-oriented evaluation; increasing participants' engagement, sense of ownership, and self-determination; and program or organizational development. They also suggest that developing professional networks and boosting morale may be evidence of process use. Of course, for process use to occur, potential users have to be engaged in the processes. Cousins and Leithwood (1993) suggest four categories of processes that were shown to result in process use: social processing, engagement, involvement, and ongoing contact. They go on to state that these activities resulted in behavioral and affective changes, such as personal and professional growth, organized reflection, and modification of practice.

This case highlights the nature of the evaluation processes of the Collaboratives for Excellence in Teacher Preparation (CETP) core evaluation in terms of the four categories presented by Cousins and Leithwood (1993). It also describes the resulting process use in terms suggested by Patton

NEW DIRECTIONS FOR EVALUATION, no. 116, Winter 2007   © Wiley Periodicals, Inc.
Published online in Wiley InterScience (www.interscience.wiley.com) • DOI: 10.1002/ev.244

(1997, 1998) and Forss, Rebien, and Carlsson (2002). Evaluation process use is often thought of in terms of the direct impact of evaluation process on nonevaluation-oriented participants; however, in this chapter, we expand the typical view of process use by examining the direct impact of a centralized core evaluation process on site evaluators, and the indirect impact on nonevaluation-oriented participants in projects. It is a multilevel look at evaluation process use and, as might be expected, shows decreasing process use as level of participation becomes less direct.

Insights into how the core evaluation stimulated use of evaluation processes from the perspectives of both the core evaluators (Lawrenz and Huffman) and one of the stakeholders (McGinnis) are provided. Various issues are explored by examining the types of participation in evaluation processes and the uses that resulted from this participation. The CETP core evaluation was a multisite evaluation of the CETP program funded by the National Science Foundation (NSF). The core evaluation was funded after the CETP program had existed for several years. Project-specific evaluations were already being conducted, and as a result, the projects themselves did not have the time and resources to develop and carry out an evaluation of the overall central aspects of the program. It was called a core evaluation because the goal was to create a centralized core of evaluation instruments and processes that would be used by all nineteen sites. The core evaluation team was committed to developing and conducting the evaluation collaboratively. This approach was used to encourage the projects to use core instruments and procedures in their own project-level evaluations as well as in the core evaluation. Projects were not required to participate in the core evaluation but were given incentives to promote participation.

A multisite, multilevel evaluation constitutes a unique opportunity to investigate evaluation process use because sites tend to participate in evaluation in different ways and ultimately use evaluation processes in varying ways. Gaventa, Creed, and Morrissey (1998) suggest that the complex funding structures of multisite evaluations highlight conflict and enhance the potential for differing perspectives across sites. They also point out that the characteristics of the people who participate in an evaluation affect their objectives and that this creates a tension in what is the most important objective of the evaluation and subsequently what might be the most appropriate methodology. Further, they suggest that a collaborative evaluation "is as much a social and political process as it is a research process" (p. 92). Additionally, Coupal and Simoneau (1998) suggest that the ability and willingness of sites to participate varies and that this could result in differential use of evaluation processes.

The CETP Program

The CETP program was designed to promote comprehensive change in the undergraduate education of future teachers by supporting cooperative,

NEW DIRECTIONS FOR EVALUATION • DOI: 10.1002/ev

multiyear efforts to increase substantially the quality and number of teachers well prepared in science and mathematics, especially members of traditionally underrepresented groups. Nationally, nineteen CETP projects were funded. Projects were funded for five years with the option for an additional three years. These were large comprehensive projects of several millions of dollars each. All of the CETP projects focused on course reform, increasing standards-based literacy of K-12 teachers, and recruitment and retention of underrepresented groups.

Core Evaluation Processes

The CETP core evaluation project was funded for three years. The first year included consensus building and instrument development along with pilot testing of processes and instruments. The second year included refinement and field testing of processes and instruments, and the last year saw final data collection. Additional information on the CETP program evaluation is available elsewhere (Lawrenz, Huffman and Gravely, in press; Lawrenz and Huffman, 2004; Lawrenz and Huffman, 2003). Cousins and Leithwood's four categories of processes (social processing, engagement, involvement, and ongoing contact; 1993) are used here to describe participation in the core evaluation processes.

There were several types of stakeholders with their own forms of participation. The stakeholders who participated the most and those who were targeted by the core evaluation to participate in the evaluation processes were the evaluators of the local projects. These stakeholders ranged from experienced evaluators to graduate students. Also included were people with science or mathematics expertise and no evaluation expertise, or vice versa. Another group of stakeholders that participated were the local project principal investigators (PIs): science, technology, engineering, or mathematics (STEM) practitioners or STEM educators. These stakeholders participated less than the local evaluators did. Their participation in the core evaluation processes was sometimes direct (for example, attending meetings) but mostly indirect, through discussion with the local evaluator. Another category of stakeholders was the local project participants. They included STEM and STEM education faculty, college students, new teachers in their first few years of teaching, and their students and principals. The participation of these stakeholders was always indirect. They would interact with the local project evaluator mostly during the data collection process, where they furnished data and discussed the data instruments and collection procedures. The final category of stakeholders was the core evaluation team members.

Social Processing. The CETP core evaluation afforded several opportunities for social processing. There were yearly meetings, hosted by the core and attended by the local evaluators and some few others such as PIs or project managers. There were yearly PI meetings hosted by NSF, which were attended by the local project PIs, evaluators, and often some other stakeholders such as students or teachers. Social processing was also fostered through the Web in the form of interactive feedback forms, a listserv, and e-mail contact. Core meetings were energetic, with the participants sharing their ideas and concerns and building consensus on how the evaluation should go forward.

At a typical PI meeting, the core evaluation would present its work to date in a plenary session with structured opportunities for feedback, such as feedback cards or embedded small group discussion and reporting out. Generally, there were "birds of a feather" discussion sessions about evaluation led by the core evaluation as well.

Engagement. In addition to the social processing, the core evaluation was very proactive in communicating with the projects using a variety of media. For example, the evaluation matrix was offered in multiple formats and the instruments were in both English and Spanish. The core also developed and sent out professionally printed handbooks and posters to remind the projects about the core evaluation processes. An especially engaging element was the videotapes of how to use the observation protocol and practice tapes of classrooms. Another example of engagement was using people from the projects as copresenters at core and PI meetings. The final set of instruments included Web-based surveys for the higher education deans and faculty members and the PIs; paper and pencil surveys for college students and K–12 principals, teachers, and students; and classroom observation protocols with Web-based data entry capacity and rubrics for scoring two classroom artifacts, activity sheets, and assessments. All of the instruments are posted at http://education.umn.edu/CAREI/CETP/default.html.

Involvement. Involvement in the evaluation process, in addition to the activities just described in terms of social processing and engagement, was extensive for the local evaluators. For example, an evaluation matrix was constructed using evaluation instruments from all of the projects and project-based teams. The final evaluation matrix listed the evaluation questions, the information needed to answer the questions, the method for gathering the data, and the source from which to obtain the data. The projects were also asked to help with pilot and field testing of the instruments. Data that were gathered from a local project were fed back to the project so that it could use the data to meet its own needs.

Ongoing Contact. Core evaluation meetings were held yearly, generally in the fall. PI meetings were held yearly in the spring. The Web site was always available, and communications were posted to the listserv regularly. Finally, personal contact with the projects through e-mail and telephone was ongoing throughout the time span of the evaluation.

Reflections on Participation in the Core Evaluation Processes

This section includes reflections from the perspective of the core evaluation, the projects, and the stakeholders.

Core Evaluation Reflection. The CETP projects were supportive and helpful in the core evaluation in spite of very busy schedules. It was clear that participating in a core evaluation, given the unique nature of each site and the various activities each project was already engaged in, was a challenge. However, all projects did their best to meet the needs of the core evaluation. Although the core evaluation supplied funds to help with data collection, many of the projects were not able to take advantage of the money because of the lack of personnel qualified to collect the data. Overall, the newer CETP projects evidenced more enthusiasm about using the core evaluation processes and instruments than the established CETPs. This was mostly because their evaluation plans were less evolved than those of the established CETP projects. Additionally, the core evaluation built consensus about the advantages of participating in the core evaluation and the quality of the instruments developed. The local project evaluators were personally supportive of the core evaluation team members. They had different needs from the core evaluators, however, and their participation resulted in an evaluation that differed from one that would have been designed without them. The final evaluation processes and instruments were reflective of the varying needs and perspectives of the projects. By the final year of the project, the core evaluation team believed that data collection was becoming somewhat routine and that the projects, especially the newer ones, were becoming accustomed to the process.

Project Reflection. One of the more established CETP projects, the Maryland Collaborative for Teacher Preparation (MCTP) project, found the core evaluation to be a valuable feature of the CETP program. After the CETPs were funded, it was brought to the attention of the projects by NSF program officers that there was a need for programwide evaluation. Pressure was being applied to the program to show overall worth, so a core evaluation was necessary. However, it was left open for the projects to shape what process would be instituted to achieve this aim. As a result of our familiarity with one another's projects, we recognized that although we shared common features, we also saw differences, which would be interesting to consider from a programwide evaluation. We also knew that the projects funded up to that point were committed to enacting their evaluation plans, and they did not desire to drop them to participate in a single, programwide evaluation. The overwhelming recommendation to NSF on the part of the projects was to have someone not associated with any particular project conduct the evaluation. The projects approved the selection of Lawrenz and Huffman.

McGinnis, who was the project representative of the MCTP in the CETP core evaluation, views the core evaluation as distinguished by the individual projects needing to set realistic boundaries for the evaluation according to their local experiences. For example, even though all the projects agreed with the core evaluators about how useful it would be to show the impact of the projects by consideration of student classroom

NEW DIRECTIONS FOR EVALUATION • DOI: 10.1002/ev

achievement data, the complications associated with this desire were significant. Projects voiced concern with both the feasibility of collecting such data and the manner in which it could be meaningfully linked in a causality analysis of the CETP projects. As a result, when the core evaluators listened to the concerns and adapted the core evaluation design to fit perceived constraints, their action was met with much approval by the projects. The core evaluators' flexibility encouraged the projects to develop an *esprit de corps* in the CETP programwide evaluation.

Left unresolved, however, was how to incorporate new data collection activities associated with the core evaluation into existing project evaluation and research activities (for examples, see McGinnis, 2003; McGinnis and others, 2002; and McGinnis and Watanabe, 1999). This problem was addressed when it was shared with the projects that participation in such data collection was optional, as determined by the individual project's circumstances. The offer of additional financial support to collect targeted core data was appreciated, but it did not completely resolve other constraints felt by the projects on collecting such data (such as in some instances adding new features to project evaluation designs). The hope was that the less-established projects would participate to a higher degree than the more-established ones, because it was felt they would have to make fewer changes to their existing project evaluation practices.

As the core evaluation proceeded, a concern emerged because it became apparent that a "gold standard" core evaluation in which every project used the same instruments and collected the same data would not happen. However, from the perspective of the projects, adapting the core evaluation to the circumstances associated with its late implementation in the program made it feasible, and thus acceptable. The flexibility of the core evaluators and the collaborative manner in which the projects participated in the process resulted in a shared vision of the core evaluation as an important and necessary endeavor that could benefit all. As experienced evaluators, the project representatives accepted the compromises to the core evaluation design. Because the projects felt they were all participating in an NSF initiative greater than their local project, a programwide evaluation was valued as adding to the totality of a CETP "story."

Stakeholder Process Use. As suggested in the introduction, process use can be quite varied. Patton (1997) suggests individual, program, or organizational changes. Forss, Rebien, and Carlsson (2002) suggest that process use includes enhancing shared understandings; supporting and reinforcing the program through intervention-oriented evaluation; increasing participants' engagement, sense of ownership, and self-determination; and program or organizational development. They also suggest that developing professional networks and boosting morale may be evidence of process use. Several examples of these types of use were apparent in the CETP core evaluation. Additionally, there were several kinds of stakeholders: the core evaluation team, evaluators of the local projects, local project PIs,

STEM and STEM education faculty, college students, and new teachers and their students and principals. We believe that the stakeholders participating in the core evaluation processes showed process use. The bulk of the process use that occurred, however, was changes in the local evaluators themselves and in their local evaluations.

One example of process use experienced by the local evaluators and PIs was the development of professional networks. Before the core evaluation, the local evaluators operated independently, but the core evaluation brought them together and a social network evolved. Many of the people who met for the first time during the CETP core evaluation are still engaged with each other and STEM evaluations. Additionally, the participants brought their own contacts into the network started by the core evaluation. An example of the external-to-internal networking was the requests we received from non-CETP projects to use the instruments. The people who requested instruments heard about the core evaluation and its instruments from the local projects.

Another example of process use was boosting of morale for local evaluators and PIs. Before the funding of the core evaluation, the local evaluators felt overburdened by NSF's increasing demands for a program evaluation. They and the PIs did not see how they could meet these increasing demands as well as meet their existing commitments. They were relieved when the core evaluation was funded, and the relief led to a boost in morale. The core evaluation also helped boost morale in that it functioned as a mediator for NSF demands on the projects. The core evaluation team was able to advocate on behalf of the CETP projects and help present a combined voice in negotiating with NSF on evaluation of the projects.

Another important example of process use was the actual collection of the evaluation data. Cousins and Leithwood (1993) suggest that there may not be a clear line between use of findings and use of processes. We suggest that in the CETP data collection there may not be a clear line between involvement in the evaluation and use of evaluation processes. We believe that because collection of data was voluntary and quite distinct from the ongoing evaluation at each site it represents process use rather than simply involvement in the evaluation.

Another powerful example of process use was enhanced shared understanding of reform instruction through development and use of the observation protocol and the surveys on reform instruction. This is an important type of process use because there are such diverse views about reform instruction. Although this effect was mostly concentrated on the local evaluators and the PIs, it also affected faculty, teachers, and their principals. Going through the training process and learning how to use the observation protocol led to an increase in shared understanding about reformed instruction. Faculty and new teachers who were observed by the local evaluators learned more about what might be expected in reform-oriented STEM classes, as the observers used the classroom observation protocol. Faculty

NEW DIRECTIONS FOR EVALUATION • DOI: 10.1002/ev

and teachers also learned what might be considered important reform instruction outcomes by examining the teacher and student surveys. Principals were also affected by the surveys because they highlighted what might be expected in the classrooms of reform-oriented STEM teachers. Additionally some of the projects used the observation protocol directly as a professional development device to stimulate discussion among participants about reform instruction.

Another example of shared understanding was in terms of research design. For all CETP projects, the core evaluation encouraged a culture of examining the impact of innovation in teacher preparation through empirical means. Engaging in the process of collecting quantitative data for evaluators who came from more interpretive philosophies led to changes in individual thinking and behavior on the part of the local site evaluators. At first, it was rather disconcerting for these individuals to relate to the quantitative data, but eventually they began to believe that the quantitative data were valuable. The process of engaging with quantitative data led some local site evaluators to rethink the range of data needed to evaluate their CETP project. Sites that attempted to collect all the core data had to change to meet the needs of the core, and there were indications that organizational procedures in local evaluations were changed as a result of the learning that occurred.

Through completing the instruments and through discussion with the local evaluators and PIs, faculty members at the local colleges and universities were stimulated to think more about interactions with their colleagues and the amount of effort they put forth in their teaching as well as their perceptions of faculty members and students from other disciplines. Faculty also gained experience collecting empirical data on instruction and in discussing the findings with the project PIs.

PIs were exposed to a range of ideas about what might be appropriate outcomes from projects of this sort through their surveys. They also learned a good deal about how to evaluate programs, strengths, and weaknesses of approaches; how to develop instruments; and how to reflect on data through the sessions at the PI meetings and indirectly through the local evaluators who were working with the core. The participation and discussions encouraged PIs to modify their programs to be more aligned with the issues covered by the evaluation questions and in the instruments.

The local evaluators, particularly the ones from the newer CETPs, developed ownership in at least some of the core evaluation processes. The core evaluation increased participants' sense of identity as a special population involved in mathematics or science teacher preparation. By being asked to contribute information on their participation in the CETP, they have demonstrated greater self-awareness as a unique and identifiable group. Because the core evaluation data collection activities were voluntary, for some participants it increased their sense of ownership and self-determination when they chose to contribute the perspective of their local CETP to a programwide evaluation. Several local evaluators also incorporated the core ideas about research design and core instruments into their own local evaluation processes. Some reported modifying the core instruments for special needs or for use in other projects. Others reported presenting ideas from the core at professional meetings.

We believe process use does not occur in a single direction, flowing only from the evaluation team to the other stakeholders. The core evaluation team was also affected by participating in the core evaluation. First, as was suggested earlier regarding the local evaluators, participation in the CETP process helped to develop professional networks for the core evaluation team. The team also experienced significant individual changes in thinking and behavior. The core team learned much more about how to facilitate discussions about evaluation, the range of evaluation expertise, different philosophical approaches to evaluation, how to build evaluation capacity, and how these aspects of evaluation interacted with the conduct of an evaluation. These changes in individual knowledge led to changes in the core evaluation processes indicative of organizational or cultural use of evaluation processes such as more individualized communication and development of more artifacts that the local projects could pull out and "hold." The challenging process of attempting to create and then get projects to use the core evaluation led us to changes in our individual thinking on the extent to which a national core evaluation is possible.

Additionally, when the members of the evaluation team conducted evaluations after the CETP core evaluation, their approaches and procedures differed because of what they had learned while participating in the CETP core evaluation processes. For example, achieving buy-in early in the life of a program is critical, as is the support of the funding agency in "encouraging" everyone to participate; acknowledgement of contrasting philosophical approaches is necessary, and compromise is inevitable; and funding agencies must be willing to be flexible about what will become the final evaluation design.

Concluding Remarks

In this example, we found that participating in evaluation processes, even ones that included social processing, engagement, involvement, and ongoing contact, was not enough to engender process use. This is supported by Gaventa, Creed, and Morrissey (1998), who suggest that the disconnect between stakeholders and project directors can lead to differential evaluation process use. We found that the stakeholders' process use was constrained by their own goals, philosophies, situations, and capacity.

The local evaluator stakeholders were interested in questions of process and meaning and were more likely to use core evaluation processes that directly aligned with what they were doing (Maxwell, 2004). They had predetermined goals or standards they wanted their participants to meet. For example, the local projects were less interested in student achievement (a more distal goal favored by the core evaluation) than behaviors of teachers prepared in their programs. This resulted in no student achievement data being collected by the core evaluation.

Use of evaluation processes was also related to the philosophical bases of the local evaluators. Local evaluators with interpretive philosophies were more affected by the interviews and discussions than the positivistic evaluators, and vice versa. However, the opportunity for the evaluators to come together and discuss these philosophical differences resulted in greater understanding and appreciation for the "other" side.

Use of evaluation processes was also related to the feasibility of the use. Projects that already had extensive evaluation plans were much less likely to be affected by participating in the core evaluation than those just beginning their local evaluation efforts. Additionally, practical issues of how to obtain random samples, time involved in conducting classroom observations, reluctant respondent groups, and so on, dictated which components of the core evaluation were used. In a sense, this led to organizational changes in procedures—one of Patton's indications of process use.

Use of evaluation processes was also related to the evaluation capacity of each site. The local evaluators varied in terms of their evaluation expertise, as did other stakeholders. Each person was differentially affected by participating in the evaluation processes, depending on their personal level of knowledge and behavior.

Overall, this example of evaluation process use amounts to a slightly different way of viewing process use. Typically, process use is viewed in terms of the impact on nonevaluator participants. In this example, we used a multisite view of process use to examine the influence of process use on local site evaluators, on other participants, and on the core team. The example compares and contrasts the theoretical aspects of how complex multisite evaluations affect evaluation process use. The example highlights some of the unique challenges, dilemmas, and issues related to evaluation process use, including philosophical perspectives, evaluation capacity, and pragmatic concerns. The CETP core evaluation is an interesting example because it was not a mandated central evaluation, but rather a voluntary example of what multiple sites might do as part of a large national evaluation.

The CETP core evaluation example presents a range of issues that may affect the complex phenomenon of evaluation process use. It highlights the need to better understand the factors that affect evaluation process use in the hope that we can design and implement evaluations in such a way as to maximize evaluation process use. By viewing process use by both stakeholders and evaluators in a large multisite national core evaluation, we are hopefully able to extend thinking about the extent to which process use occurs in complex multisite situations, and more importantly, to help program evaluations promote more process use in the future.

References

Coupal, F. P., and Simoneau, M. "A Case Study of Participatory Evaluation in Haiti." In E. Whitmore (ed.), *Understanding and Practicing Participatory Evaluation. New Directions for Evaluation,* no. 80. San Francisco: Jossey-Bass, 1998.

Cousins, J. B., and Leithwood, K. A. "Enhancing Knowledge Utilization as a Strategy for School Improvement." *Knowledge: Creation, Diffusion, Utilization.* 1993, *14*(3), 305–333.

Forss, K., Rebien, C. C., and Carlsson, J. "Process Use of Evaluations: Types of Use That Precede Lessons Learned and Feedback." *Evaluation,* 2002, *8*(1), 29–45.

Gaventa, J., Creed, V., and Morrissey, J. "Scaling up: Participatory Monitoring and Evaluation of a Federal Empowerment Program." In E. Whitmore (ed.), *Understanding and Practicing Participatory Evaluation. New Directions for Evaluation,* no. 80. San Francisco: Jossey-Bass, 1998.

Lawrenz, F., and Huffman, D. "Multi-Site Participatory Program Evaluation." *American Journal of Evaluation,* 2003, *24*(4), 471–482.

Lawrenz, F., and Huffman, D. "Using Multi-Site Core Evaluation to Provide 'Scientific' Evidence." *Canadian Journal of Program Evaluation,* 2004, *19*(2), 17–36.

Lawrenz, F., Huffman, D., and Gravely, A. "Impact of the Collaboratives for Excellence in Teacher Preparation Program." *Journal of Research in Science Teaching,* in press.

Maxwell, J. "Causal Explanation, Qualitative Research, and Scientific Inquiry in Education." *Educational Researcher,* 2004, *33*(2), 3–11.

McGinnis, J. R. "College Science, Mathematics, and Methods Teaching Faculty Talk About Science and Mathematics: An Examination of Faculty Discourse in a Reform-Based Teacher Preparation Program." *International Journal of Mathematics and Science Education,* 2003, *1,* 5–38.

McGinnis, J. R., and Watanabe, T. "The Use of Research to Inform the Evaluation of the Maryland Collaborative for Teacher Preparation." *Journal of Mathematics and Science: Collaborative Explorations,* 1999, *2*(1), 91–104.

McGinnis, J. R., and others. "Undergraduates' Attitudes and Beliefs of Subject Matter and Pedagogy Measured Periodically in a Reform-Based Mathematics and Science Teacher Preparation Program." *Journal of Research in Science Teaching,* 2002, *39*(8), 713–737.

Patton, M. Q. *Utilization-Focused Evaluation: The New Century Text* (3rd ed.). Thousand Oaks, Calif.: Sage, 1997.

Patton, M. Q. "Discovering Process Use." *Evaluation,* 1998, *4,* 225–233.

FRANCES LAWRENZ *is the associate vice president for research and a professor of educational psychology at the University of Minnesota.*

DOUGLAS HUFFMAN *is an associate professor of science education at the University of Kansas.*

J. RANDY MCGINNIS *is a professor of science education at the University of Maryland.*

This case narrative discusses the author's experience with an evaluation process use with HIV/AIDS nonprofits in Southern Africa. The case narrative highlights the various ways in which an evaluator can incorporate process use, and how the decision to employ process use often relies on the evaluator's ethical decisions.

Process Use: A Case Narrative from Southern Africa

Donna Podems

As an evaluator who works in Latin America, Asia, and Africa, I have witnessed poverty that is deplorable, squatter camps that have no toilets and are home to thousands of people, houses made from tin cans, schools with no books, and sick children with treatable diseases. I have seen people living with HIV/AIDS who are treated so shockingly by their family and community that it is hard to keep the horror from showing in my eyes. I make these observations as an evaluator who is often in the position of judging the results of social interventions that are intended to influence these social ills.

The funding agency that hires me to evaluate these interventions often requires an evaluation report, one that frequently has restricted uses. After spending days, weeks, and sometimes months collecting data for a report that, in the best-case scenario, a few people will use, I found myself questioning the utility of my work.

As a practicing evaluator in these contexts with these experiences, I began to recognize the value of an evaluation process that leads to a final report. For me, process use ethically justifies not only my work, but often the time and other resources that I take from those involved in the evaluation process—the time and resources that are not used directly to influence social ills.

Michael Patton provides the process use description given here: "Process use refers to and is indicated by individual changes in thinking and behavior, and program or organizational changes in procedures and culture,

NEW DIRECTIONS FOR EVALUATION, no. 116, Winter 2007 © Wiley Periodicals, Inc.
Published online in Wiley InterScience (www.interscience.wiley.com) • DOI: 10.1002/ev.245

87

which occur among those involved in evaluation as a result of the learning that occurs during the evaluation process" (Patton, 1997, p. 90).

For me, process use involves any useful learning for any person involved in the evaluation that takes place during an evaluation, planned or unplanned, intentional or unintentional, that is not directly related to the evaluation findings. In my experience, process use begins the moment I am contacted to conduct an evaluation and may have lasting influences long after I am gone.

This case narrative illustrates an example of the intrinsic worth of a process use to an evaluation practitioner and those she comes into contact with during the evaluation.

The Case of an HIV/AIDS Program Evaluation in Southern Africa

A U.S. organization (the donor) that funds social intervention programs in Africa contacted me to conduct an evaluation for an HIV/AIDS program that they currently fund in a Southern African country. The donor explained that they believed a consortium model would offer better services than individual nonprofits to people infected and affected by HIV/AIDS.

Thus, for the past few years, the donor had funded several HIV/AIDS consortia in Southern Africa. During my initial contact with the donor, they explained that they wanted to determine the extent of the consortium model's usefulness. Several weeks later, the terms of reference arrived and included this question to be addressed: Did the HIV/AIDS consortium have an impact on the services provided by consortium members to people affected and infected with HIV/AIDS? During my initial conversation with the donor, I began as I always do, by asking general questions such as what data they had already collected. I explored the donor's intended evaluation use: What did they intend to do with the results? And I asked open-ended questions querying their understanding of impact: What criteria and standards did they employ to make impact judgments (Patton, 1997; Greene, 2000)? These and other questions resulted in lengthy discussions that determined a few fundamental facts: (1) the donor and the implementer had collected little program data over the past two years; (2) the donor intended to use the evaluation results to influence its funding decisions yet; and (3) the donor's criteria and standards for determining impact were unclear. The donor did state that if the consortium approach did not appear to be adding value, it would cease the consortium's funding and rethink the consortium model.

These initial discussions left me confounded on three levels. First, I was not clear what specific changes the donor expected to see as a result of the two-year funding cycle. Second, I wondered if we were defining impact in the same manner. Third, I questioned why the donor decided to ask for an impact evaluation as opposed to an evaluation approach that tested the program's evaluability or sought to understand the program's implementation process.

On the basis of these additional questions, I encouraged the donor to engage with me regarding evaluation and its potential various uses. I assumed that if the donor understood the range of evaluation options that existed, it would choose an evaluation approach that was perhaps more fitting (that is, would be designed to produce more useful findings) for the current context.

Therefore the process use began during the evaluation's conceptualization. Specifically, I intended that the process used to define the evaluation approach would increase the donor's understanding and knowledge regarding evaluation and its potential benefits. This would then lead to an evaluation that would yield useful results for its intended user, the donor. Although the engagement that took place prior to implementation of the evaluation resulted in various discussions regarding evaluation, the process did not result in any obvious or documented use.

Because I have limited space, I will truncate the ensuing discussion and proceed to its end result: whereas I explored several evaluation options with the donor, the donor ultimately decided that it required the two-year-old program (that had little monitoring data and no previous evaluations) to have an impact evaluation implemented in ten days (five for data gathering).

So what happened next? I did what I imagine many other practitioners do in this situation: I began the evaluation.

Evaluation Process. The evaluation process included discussing the methodology, preparing for, and conducting the evaluation. We now turn to a summary of these processes.

Methodology. The donor determined that I should interview the three consortium nonprofits and their beneficiaries. Further, the donor felt that semistructured interviews with the program staff and group interviews with the beneficiaries would generate sufficient data. I developed general interview tools based on the program documents and discussions held with the donor.

Evaluation Preparation. The U.S. donor organization provided documentation regarding the program design and its intended results; from these documents, I identified two fundamental facts. First, the program intended to provide people affected and infected by HIV/AIDS with improved access to HIV/AIDS-related services. Second, the donor's program theory appeared to be that if HIV/AIDS service organizations worked together then people affected and infected by HIV/AIDS would receive increased access to services.

Based on this theory, the donor's program logic resulted in joining three HIV/AIDS nonprofit organizations that furnished various and noncompeting services to those affected and infected by HIV/AIDS. The donor's intended result was that a person receiving services from one of the three nonprofits would then be aware of, and have access to, the services provided by the other two nonprofits. Because the donor had not yet clearly defined impact, I surmised from this logic and the evaluation question that perhaps the donor considered increased access to services as impact; or maybe not.

To form the consortium, the donor chose three local nonprofits that provided fundamentally different services to their infected or affected HIV/AIDS clients. The donor did not describe (or at least did not give me) documents that detailed the process for choosing the nonprofits. From conjecture, I surmised that the criteria included that the nonprofits had to provide services to both infected and affected persons and offer noncompeting services.

Finally, the documentation I had featured vague descriptions that afforded little insight into the nonprofits themselves. The documents did state that nonprofit A provided training in two areas: (1) basic knowledge of and prevention and spread of HIV/AIDS and (2) small business development. The documents further noted that nonprofit B was a men's organization that promoted women's rights by encouraging the formation of men's groups in small communities. These men's groups addressed issues related to HIV/AIDS and violence against women. The third organization, nonprofit C, was described as a group that supported women through encouraging self-growth and capacity development. I did not identify nonprofit C's link to HIV/AIDS. The donor's consortium model included designating one organization, nonprofit A, as the lead nonprofit responsible for all funding monies and coordination among the three organizations.

Evaluation Process in Brief. When I arrived in country, nonprofit A informed me that they had not organized interviews or informed the other two consortium members that I would be in the country, because they did not realize I was arriving that week. Throughout the week, nonprofit A managed to organize a few interviews with each consortium's director and one group interview with one beneficiary group.

I quickly surmised that the possible data that I would be able to gather would most likely not result in evaluation findings useful to the donor. Thus, I critically reflected on what strategies I could use to ensure that, at the very least, the implementer and its beneficiaries would gain some use from this evaluation process. In other words, because I was concerned that this evaluation report had limited potential direct use for the donor or indirect use for the nonprofits, I was determined to ensure that, at the very least, the time I spent implementing the evaluation resulted in some tangible use.

Process Use. The evaluation's process resulted in various impacts for stakeholders. We now turn to a summary of them.

Promoting a Shared Understanding of Evaluation. Process use often varies from evaluation to evaluation, and from evaluator to evaluator. In most evaluations that I implement, I attempt to set aside time to explain the evaluation process to those being evaluated or taking part in the evaluation process. I often describe the evaluation's intended purpose and use, and what I understand will happen with regard to the findings and final report. In this case, I first asked the nonprofit's directors for their understanding of this evaluation.

NEW DIRECTIONS FOR EVALUATION • DOI: 10.1002/ev

Though each nonprofit's director understood that I was an evaluator sent to evaluate their program and the word *judgment* appeared to be on everyone's lips, the words *empirical data* collection did not feature in any of these conversations. In separate conversations, I asked the nonprofits' directors to explain what they thought happened during an evaluation. In their own way, the nonprofit directors all gave the same explanation: I (the evaluator) would make a judgment based on my opinion and then share this "finding" with the donor.

Believing that evaluation should be empowering (or at the very least not disempowering), I decided that each nonprofit director should at a minimum understand this evaluation's purpose, its processes, and how the judgments, if any, would be made. Even if this knowledge did not change the evaluation's intended use or usefulness from the nonprofits' perspective, it would enable (empower) the nonprofit directors to engage in this evaluation process and understand its purpose. Further, for each nonprofit director I offered a short explanation to facilitate his or her understanding that an evaluation's "judgment" was (or should be) based on empirical data.

Specifically, I spent time with each nonprofit director and explained (1) the three evaluation purposes (judgment, knowledge, and program improvement); (2) this evaluation's purpose; (3) my scope of work; and (4) some general research terms relevant to the evaluation process and to the nonprofit. These conversations appeared to elicit genuine interest and have perceived value for the nonprofits. The discussions with each director lasted around twenty to forty-five minutes, and the three directors had three responses to these conversations.

For example, I had the shortest conversation with nonprofit A's director, who engaged with me primarily on one topic: this evaluation. She focused our discussion by asking multiple questions regarding this evaluation, how data should be gathered, how the data would be used, and how the findings related to her continued funding. Thus her interest focused on better understanding this evaluation and its purpose. The interview with nonprofit B's director mainly focused on data credibility. For example, the director supplied ample details of his nonprofit, its values, its dreams, and its accomplishments. Once the director completed his in-depth explanation of his nonprofit, he asked if I was going to use his statements in the report.

I explained that I needed to verify his statements, and he explained that (1) there were few reports and (2) I could not speak to his beneficiaries because he did not organize visits. I clarified that if I could not verify his statements, I could not use them in an evaluation report. This led to a lengthy discussion underpinned by his concern (confusion?) as to why his word was not "good enough" for the report. Ironically, it appeared that because he believed I would form an opinion of my own he too should be able to provide his own opinion and it would be of equal value.

This led to a discussion regarding an evaluation's empirical nature and the differences between empirical and anecdotal statements. His concluding statement indicated that, though he was still confused, he also appeared enlightened: "You know, we get evaluations and outsiders a lot and it seems to me that they just use their opinion to decide to give us money or not, which is OK. I know you explain the difference about these things and it's good to know . . . still, I think outsiders just make an opinion, but now I think it's important to ask them how they formed this or that opinion . . ."

The director of nonprofit C concentrated our conversation on two topics: (1) this evaluation and (2) general evaluation questions. As a result of this discussion, she asked, "I think, well why aren't we doing an improvement evaluation? We could really use someone to help us streamline our program . . . but you know what we do is really good. I mean we do great work, but it could be streamlined."

These examples demonstrated how the evaluation process can impart useful knowledge. First, the process gave the directors practical evaluation knowledge relevant to their context. Second, their newly gained knowledge can now be used to potentially influence future evaluations. These benefits are not concrete. For example, this knowledge did not enable the directors to influence, but instead merely understand, this evaluation. However, I argue the usefulness from this standpoint: imagine not understanding a process that is not only happening to you but whose results could have quite negative consequences (that is, a cut in funding) on your program; then imagine what can happen when you gain this understanding.

Further, these examples demonstrated that an evaluation process imparts useful, empowering knowledge offered at no extra cost and with little additional time for the evaluation. In-depth or brief, formal or informal, each conversation created space for learning among the nonprofit directors. The next example presents another type of process use.

Clarifying the Program Goal. During the evaluation process, it became clear that the nonprofits had an understanding differing from the donor's regarding the program and its intended goal. The discussions surrounding evaluation had perceived and potential process use, but the second identified process use—clarifying the program goal—resulted in a tangible result.

With field days relatively clear of planned interviews, I was allowed time for lengthy conversation with the three nonprofits to explore their actual and intended results. Although I was careful not to monopolize their day (after all, I recognized that they were most likely overworked, overburdened, and overtired nonprofit staff), I did engage with each nonprofit regarding the perception of the program's intent, the actual results, and the intended goal.

The nonprofits' responses consistently led our conversation toward defining *consortium*. For example, I introduced my first question by stating that the donor sought to understand how the consortium influenced changes in the services provided to people infected or affected by HIV/AIDS. This is often where the question stopped—at the introduction—because each nonprofit's director expressed surprise at being judged as a consortium.

Directors and various staff members stated in various ways that the nonprofits did not work together to achieve results, and each should, therefore, be judged on its own merits.

Of the three nonprofits, not one thought the donor funded their nonprofit as a consortium model designed to produce collective results. Rather, the nonprofits thought the donor organized the three groups as part of a funding mechanism. For example, nonprofit A did not view itself as the coordinating body but rather the mechanism for payment for the three nonprofits.

I initiated the unintended (that is, not specified in the methodology) open-ended and exploratory conversation as a result of the nonprofits' bewilderment regarding the evaluation's question. On the basis of my understanding, I explained to each nonprofit that the donor intended to determine if the HIV/AIDS implementer's consortium (I emphasized consortium) had any impact on services for people affected or infected with HIV/AIDS. I elaborated that the donor was not interested in the individual organizations per se, but their results as a collective unit.

Though the nonprofits understood the consortium concept, and that the three nonprofits were in a consortium, they defined the consortium concept differently than the donor did. The donor explained that the three nonprofits were in a consortium to produce results; the nonprofits explained that the consortium was merely for funding purposes.

It was after this discussion that the nonprofits realized the funding would be continued only if they could demonstrate, at the very least, that they had worked together to provide services to people who were HIV/AIDS infected and affected. Further, two of the three nonprofits thought the funding was a grant. In other words, two nonprofits thought the funding was based on accountability of funds, not results.

In this example, the evaluation process resulted in the nonprofits understanding that the donor's expectations and consortium definition drastically differed from their own. As a direct result of this clarification, the three nonprofits met the day that I left the country to discuss whether and how to move forward with the donor's intended consortium model.

Learning About the Program. For the final field day, nonprofit A managed to organize one group interview with a women's group. Nonprofit A, through consultants, offered this women's group business advice for their small craft enterprise. The nonprofit's director insisted on accompanying me to the site visit, where I conducted an interview of slightly more than two hours with seven women. The director stated that because the nonprofit used consultants to work with the group, this meeting would give her an opportunity to interact with them as well.

Owing to nonprofit A's director being present at the interview (by her insistence), she directly heard the feedback provided by the various women. Thus, regardless of whether or not she ever saw the final report or what was in the report, she gained valuable insight from listening to the women's group. For example, the director stated, ". . . But it was interesting to me because it was interesting to hear what the women said about needing more help with marketing. . . . They seemed happy to receive our help, and they want more help, but now I think I understand that we need to focus more on helping them to sell their crafts . . ."

Even though the donor was the intended audience for these data, the nonprofit's director became an additional unintended audience. As a direct result of being present at the interview, she had access to data that she otherwise would not have heard. It is possible, considering her statement, that she would then use these data to perhaps positively influence the nonprofit's services.

Giving Voice to Beneficiaries. The evaluation process use extended to the nonprofit's beneficiaries, a women's group, through a purposefully designed interview process. This included (1) using open-ended questions that encouraged unbounded discussion; (2) clearly explaining that I was speaking with them because I thought their perceptions were important; and (3) explicitly stating how I would use their answers to report to the donor. Here are a few details.

The entire interview process lasted slightly more than two hours. For the first thirty minutes or so, I asked specific, descriptive questions mostly addressed to the group's leader. She supplied information regarding the services that the nonprofit provided and a few examples of how that service assisted the women's group.

During the next thirty to forty minutes, I asked open-ended probing questions such as, "What else can the group tell me?" thus encouraging the women to think and discuss their answers among themselves. This question in itself does not necessarily lead to process use, but allocating ample time for the women to explore their answers among themselves led to in-depth discussion relevant to their women's group.

For example, though the group noted few changes related to the non-profit's assistance, the question sparked a lengthy discussion among group members (approximately twenty minutes) regarding what was different, but not in relation to the nonprofit's assistance. Instead, the women discussed issues such as how the group's size had changed and why, and how the group was selling the same crafts but maybe they should change what they sold, followed by a finance discussion that the group leader abruptly ended. These data were not useful for the report, but the women, judging from their enthusiastic discussion, appeared to benefit from the discussion.

As the evaluator, I had consciously allowed time for the women's group to benefit by giving the women time to discuss issues they found important. By not rushing or redirecting their thought process to focus only on my data needs, the process allowed, and even encouraged, the women to generate useful data that benefited their group.

After approximately an hour or so, and an immeasurable amount of tea and cookies furnished by the women's group, I began asking broader questions, attempting to gain an understanding of what assistance or results, if any, the women perceived as significant. To gather these data, I asked questions such as, "I am going write a report that is going to be read by the donor that provides the funds for this program; I need to know what you want me to tell them." For prompts, I used iterations of this question such as, What do you want the staff to know? What do you want the donor to know? What do you want me to write? How do you want me to write that? What else do you want me to tell the donor for you?

Prior to the last question I asked, "Do you have any questions for me?" After all, it seemed only fair; I had just spent nearly two hours asking them questions. The group responded with a flurry of personal questions that I answered. I then followed up with my last question: "Do you have anything else to tell me that I forgot to ask?" Of all the questions asked, the last question generated the most data.

At the beginning of the interview, I informed the group of the reasons for the interview, mainly that I would take the information back to the donor. It was as if, in the beginning, the women doubted that their voices would actually be heard by the donor; their answers were short and appeared to be standard (for instance, they stated they would like additional funds and resources). However, by the end of the interview, it appeared that the women believed I truly did value what they said. For example, they gave more specific, and seemingly more thoughtful, answers generated after group discussion. For me, this was a significant process use, as the group leader explained: "Are you really going to write what we say in the report? You need to tell the donor . . . it makes me feel good that you value what we say. . . . You are a very nice person to listen to us, we don't get many visitors and we think the nonprofit could do more for us. . . . We are proud that you chose to listen to us and spent so much time with us."

Guided primarily by my feminist evaluation theory and ethics, this process resulted in two benefits (Sielbeck-Bowen and others, 2002). First, it allowed a marginalized, "poor" women's group infected and affected by HIV/AIDS to know that an "outsider" listens to them, values what they think, and gives them a voice. Second, the conversations and discussions encouraged the women to analyze and discuss issues and ideas that would hopefully result in positive changes for their project—changes that they could make.

How It All Ended. The donor hired me to conduct an impact evaluation; that is what the donor wanted. Given that I found no impact and had very few data, my first report to the donor reflected the lessons described here and gave detailed information regarding the data collection and analysis process, as well as conclusions and recommendations. For example, one recommendation suggested that the donor furnish a facilitator to assist the nonprofits in engaging and developing their consortium. I presented various examples to support this recommendation, but the donor rejected the suggestion, stating that I was not to comment on the donor; I was only allowed to comment on the program.

Ultimately, the donor rejected the report, stating that it did "not read like an impact evaluation" and told me to rewrite the report so that "it was an impact evaluation." I asked for clarity on what they meant, but none was forthcoming. I rewrote a short report with no data or comments related to the donor and stated that no impact had been determined during the evaluation. The donor accepted the report. Curious to know if the report had been used, approximately three months following submission of the final report, I followed through with one e-mail and one phone message to the donor. The donor did not return the call or respond to the e-mail.

Did the donor, the nonprofits, or their beneficiaries use the report? I am not sure. Did anyone benefit from the evaluation report? I am not sure about that either, although I somehow doubt it. From my value-laden standpoint, I would suggest that any time I take resources—whether staff time or money—from a nonprofit, I should ensure that there is some use. After all, a nonprofit is providing services to "poor" and "marginalized" people to whom the government and private sector cannot or will not provide services.

As an evaluator, sometimes process use is all I have to offer.

Implications for Evaluation. Yet what are the implications of this case narrative for an evaluator and for evaluation? I intended to demonstrate two very different insights regarding process use. The first lessons revolve around process use itself. Even when process use is intended, it does not necessarily happen, as demonstrated by the interaction with the donor. Process use does not necessarily imply that additional time or resources are needed; conversations that last twenty minutes can result in useful learning. Process use does not necessarily require lengthy planning and often relies on the evaluator's accessing his or her own readily available skills and knowledge. Finally, process use is not always apparent; this case narrative does not necessarily exhaust all the process use that may have occurred of which I was not aware.

The second lessons revolve around the evaluator's role and decision-making processes used during an evaluation. An evaluation process use may be a result of other causes, but this case narrative illustrates that when an evaluator believes evaluations should be useful and learning is important, the evaluator assigns herself or himself the educator and communicator role (that is, roles not covered in the scope of work). The decision, however, to place oneself in this role is ethical. For example, I placed myself in these roles on the basis of my expectations of an evaluation process and my own ethics. These personal ethics guided each and every decision that I made to ensure process use.

In other words, I actively and purposefully chose to fill the educator and communicator role; I actively chose to impart a voice to those who are disempowered; and I actively chose to offer knowledge that is empowering. I made these decisions from my ethics, not from my scope of work. If I had not filled these roles, the evaluation would still have taken place and the final evaluation report would still have been written with the same findings.

Yet here is the dilemma. I was not paid to fill these three roles, and it was not implied in my contract, or discussed with the donor agency that hired me or with the nonprofits that I evaluated, that I would fulfill them. I made these decisions on the basis of my own ethics and understanding of the purpose of an evaluation. As an evaluator, I chose to recognize the value of process use; others might argue that I overstepped my bounds.

References

Greene, J. C. "Understanding Social Programs Through Evaluation." In N. K. Denzin and Y. S. Lincoln (eds.), *Handbook of Qualitative Research* (2nd ed.). Thousand Oaks, Calif.: Sage, 2000.

Patton, M. Q. *Utilization-Focused Evaluation* (3rd ed.). Thousand Oaks, Calif.: Sage, 1997.

Sielbeck-Bowen, K., and others. "Exploring Feminist Evaluation: The Ground from Which We Rise." In D. Siegart and S. Brisolara (eds.), *Feminist Evaluation: Explorations and Experiences. New Directions for Evaluation*, no. 96. San Francisco: Jossey-Bass, 2002.

DONNA PODEMS is a research fellow at the Centre for Research on Science and Technology, Stellenbosch, South Africa, and serves as a senior evaluation facilitator for Macro International.

7

Process use is best understood and used as a sensitizing concept. Judging the concept's meaningfulness through the lens of operationalization misconstrues its utility. This closing chapter also examines what other chapters in this volume reveal about process use as a sensitizing concept.

Process Use as a Usefulism

Michael Quinn Patton

Linguistic pundit William Safire devoted a *New York Times* column to defining the "pre-autumn of life." What, he pondered, is "middle age"? He considered several operational definitions, judging each inadequate. Ironically, the more precise the definition (for example, forty-five to sixty), the more problematic its general utility. He concluded that the inherent ambiguity of the term *middle life* and the resulting implication that each of us must define it in context made it not a euphemism but rather a "usefulism" (Safire, 2007). I shall argue that the concept *process use* is a usefulism. Safire's playful term is what qualitative inquirers call a sensitizing concept.

Process use refers to changes in attitude, thinking, and behavior that result from participating in an evaluation. Process use includes individual learnings from evaluation involvement as well as effects on program functioning and organizational culture. Process use is distinguished from findings use. Table 7.2, later in this chapter, lists six types of process use.

To appreciate the significance of this *New Directions* volume, consider the conclusion of Cousins and Shulha (2006) after reviewing the utilization literature for the *Handbook of Evaluation*: "Possibly the most significant development of the past decade in both research and evaluation communities has been a more general acceptance that *how* we work with clients and practitioners can be as meaningful and consequential as *what* we learn from our methods" (emphasis in original; p. 277).

NEW DIRECTIONS FOR EVALUATION, no. 116, Winter 2007   © Wiley Periodicals, Inc.
Published online in Wiley InterScience (www.interscience.wiley.com) • DOI: 10.1002/ev.246

A State of Confusion?

Harnar and Preskill analyze an open-ended survey item aimed at discerning evaluators' understanding of process use. They "question whether the term is confusing to many evaluators, given that the field uses the term *process* in describing the process *of* evaluation and process evaluations." However, their data show that only 3 of their 481 respondents actually confused process evaluation with process use. Overall, I was encouraged that so many respondents did so well with the concept. They found that those who expressed greatest clarity about process use were more experienced evaluators who employ participatory, user-focused, and capacity-building approaches, which makes sense because such stakeholder-involving approaches emphasize learning from an evaluation.

Readers can decide for themselves how much the Harnar and Preskill analysis reveals confusion versus substantial understanding of the core concept. I am actually reassured by their findings. Moreover, their construct validity concerns set an excellent context for Amo and Cousins (Chapter One) on operationalizing process use. At the 2006 AEA conference session that led to this volume, Harnar was especially critical of the lack of operationalization of the concept. So what did Amo and Cousins find about operationalization?

Operationalizing Process Use

Amo and Cousins define operationalization "as the process of translating an abstract construct into concrete measures for the purpose of observing the construct." This constitutes a well-established, scholarly approach to empirical inquiry with which few trained social scientists would quibble. I do quibble, however. I am not worried about the lack of a general operational definition of process use. I have offered process use as a *sensitizing concept* in the tradition of qualitative inquiry, not as an operational concept in the tradition of quantitative research. I would like to explore this distinction and its implications for understanding process use.

The *Encyclopedia of Social Science Research Methods,* in an entry on operationalization, affirms the scientific goal of standardizing definitions of key concepts. It notes that concepts vary in their degree of abstractness, using as an illustration the concepts human capital versus education versus number of years of schooling as moving from high abstraction to operationalization. The entry then observes: "Social science theories that are more abstract are usually viewed as being the most useful for advancing knowledge. However, as concepts become more abstract, reaching agreement on appropriate measurement strategies becomes more difficult" (Mueller, 2004, p. 162).

Interesting. Abstraction is *useful* for advancing knowledge and building theory. Process use is abstract, to be sure, and its very quality of abstraction makes it difficult to reach agreement on how to measure (operationalize) it.

The entry continues: "Social science researchers do not use [operationalization] as much as in the past, primarily because of the negative connotation associated with its use in certain contexts" (p. 162).

What is this? Operationalization has negative connotations and the term's use is in decline? The entry discusses the controversy surrounding the relationship between the concept of intelligence and the operationalization of intelligence through intelligence tests, including the classic critique that the splendidly abstract and sensitizing concept of intelligence has been reduced by psychometricians to what intelligence tests measure.

"Operationalization as a value has been criticized because it reduces the concept to the operations used to measure it, what is sometimes called 'raw empiricism.' As a consequence, few researchers define their concepts by how they are operationalized. Instead, nominal definitions are used . . . and measurement of the concepts is viewed as a distinct and different activity. Researchers realized that measures do not perfectly capture concepts, although . . . the goal is to obtain measures that validly and reliably capture the concepts" (p. 162).

It appears that there is something of a conundrum here, some tension between social science theorizing and empirical research. This tension is reflected in the extensive and quite valuable table constructed by Amo and Cousins summarizing studies of process use. It looks to me like a great deal of what they report in Table 1.1 as "operationalization" actually references nominal, rather than operational, definitions.

A second entry in the *Encyclopedia of Social Science Research Methods* sheds more light on this issue. "Operationalism began life in the natural sciences . . . and is a variant of positivism. It specifies that scientific concepts must be linked to instrumental procedures in order to determine their values. . . . In the social sciences, operationalism enjoyed a brief spell of acclaim. . . . Operationalism remained fairly uncontroversial while the natural and social sciences were dominated by POSITIVISM but was an apparent casualty of the latter's fall from grace" (Williams, 2004, pp. 768–769; emphasis in the original).

The entry elaborates three problems with operationalization. First, "underdetermination" is the problem of determining "if testable propositions fully operationalize a theory" (p. 769). Examples include concepts such as homelessness, poverty, and alienation that have variable meanings according to the social context. What "homeless" means varies historically and sociologically. A second problem is that objective scholarly definitions may not capture the subjective definition of those who experience something. Poverty offers an example: What one person considers poverty, another may view as a pretty decent life. The Northwest Area Foundation, which has as its mission "poverty alleviation," has struggled trying to operationalize poverty for outcomes evaluation; moreover, they found that many quite poor people in states such as Iowa and Montana, who fit every official definition of being in poverty, do not even see themselves as poor, much less "in poverty." Third is the problem of disagreement among social scientists about how to define and operationalize key concepts. The second and third problems are related in that one researcher may use a local and context-specific definition to solve the second problem, but this context-specific definition is likely to be different from and conflict with the definition used by other researchers inquiring in other contexts.

One way to address problems of operationalization is to treat process use as a sensitizing concept and abandon the search for a standardized and universal operational definition. This means that any specific empirical study of process use would generate a definition that fit the specific context for and purpose of the study, but operational definitions would be expected to vary. More on the implications of that later. First, let us look at process use as a sensitizing concept.

Process Use as a Sensitizing Concept

Sociologist Herbert Blumer (1954) is credited with originating the idea of "sensitizing concept" to orient fieldwork. Sensitizing concepts include notions like victim, stress, stigma, and learning organization that can provide some initial direction to a study as one inquires into how the concept is given meaning in a particular place or set of circumstances (Schwandt, 2001). The observer moves between the sensitizing concept and the real world of social experience, giving shape and substance to the concept and elaborating the conceptual framework with varied manifestations of the concept. Such an approach recognizes that although the specific manifestations of social phenomena vary by time, space, and circumstance, the sensitizing concept is a container for capturing, holding, and examining these manifestations to better understand patterns and implications.

Evaluators commonly use sensitizing concepts to inform their understanding of a situation. Consider the notion of context. Any particular evaluation is designed within some context and we are admonished to take context into account, be sensitive to context, and watch out for changes in context. But what is context? Not long ago, an animated discussion on EVALTALK explored this issue. Systems thinkers posited that system boundaries are inherently arbitrary, so defining what is within the immediate scope of an evaluation versus what is within its surrounding context is inevitably arbitrary, but the distinction is still useful. Indeed, being intentional about deciding what is in the immediate realm of action of an evaluation and what is in the enveloping context can be an illuminating exercise—and stakeholders might well differ in their perspectives. In that sense, the idea of *context* is another usefulism, or a sensitizing concept. Those on EVALTALK seeking an operational definition of context ranted in some frustration about the ambiguity, vagueness, and diverse meanings of what they ultimately decided was a useless and vacuous concept. Why? Because it had not been (and could not be) operationally defined—and they displayed a low tolerance for the ambiguity that is inherent in such sensitizing concepts.

A sensitizing concept raises consciousness about something and alerts us to watch out for it within a specific context. This is what the concept of process use does. It says things are happening to people and changes are taking place in programs and organizations as evaluation takes place, especially when stakeholders are involved in the process. Watch out for those things. Pay attention. Something important may be happening. The process may be producing outcomes quite apart from findings. Think about what is going on. Help the people in the situation pay attention to what is going on, if that seems appropriate and useful. Perhaps even make process use a matter of intention.

But do not judge the maturity and utility of the concept by whether it has "achieved" a standardized and universally accepted operational definition. Judge it instead by its utility in sensitizing us to the variety of outcomes that an evaluation may produce beyond findings. This means that specific studies of process use generate their own operational definitions as appropriate. Over time, many empirical studies may use the same or similar operational definitions. Periodically, syntheses and comparisons are undertaken, as in the Amo and Cousins exemplar in this volume. We can learn a great deal from how researchers define process use, whether operationally (deductively and quantitatively), nominally (as a sensitizing concept), or inductively (exploring emergent meanings and manifestations). What I am arguing against is the notion that arriving at some standard operational definition is the desired target, some kind of "achievement" indicating maturity, consensus, shared understanding, and professional acceptance.

Specific Outcomes of Process Use

When I introduced *process use* (Patton, 1997), I suggested four outcomes that might occur from involvement in an evaluation: (1) enhancing understandings about the program among those involved (for example, the program logic model); (2) reinforcing the program intervention; (3) increasing commitment and facilitating the learning of those involved; and (4) program and organizational development. Harnar and Preskill refer to these as "indicators" of process use, but they are not indicators at all in the operational measurement sense. They are specific sensitizing categories within the broader sensitizing concept of process use. In the forthcoming revision of *Utilization-Focused Evaluation* (Patton, in press), I add two more domains: (5) infusing evaluation thinking into an organization's culture and (6) instrumentation effects (that is, what gets measured gets done). Table 7.2 offers more details on these six manifestations of process use.

The inspiration for the process use domain of infusing evaluative thinking into an organization's culture is the IDRC example that is presented in Carden and Earl's Chapter Four in this volume. In consulting with the International Development Research Centre (IDRC), I have observed up close the effort to make evaluative thinking a centerpiece of the organization's culture and an explicit part of IDRC's accountability framework. In so doing, they have attempted to operationalize evaluative thinking, with mixed results. Why? Because *evaluative thinking is also a sensitizing concept.* The rolling Project Completion Report process they describe is, in my judgment, a stellar exemplar of process use. People throughout the organization, at various levels and across program areas, interview each other to complete reports on implementation lessons and project outcomes. Those involved ask evaluative questions, probe for results, articulate "lessons" (another sensitizing concept), and enhance communications throughout the organization. The interviews generate reflections and reactions—*instrumentation effects.*

Another example of instrumentation effects is the learning that occurs during a focus group. Wiebeck and Dahlgren (2007) found that focus group participants engage in problem solving as they respond to questions. Sharing what they think and know, participants generate new knowledge as a group that can affect individual knowledge and beliefs, and even subsequent behavior. Expressing disagreement can also stimulate learning as participants challenge each other, defend their own views, and sometimes modify their viewpoint. Thus, even though quotations from focus groups constitute evaluation findings, the interactions and learnings in the group constitute process use.

The survey question analyzed by Harnar and Preskill is a premier example of instrumentation effects. The purpose of the question was to find out "what process use looks like" to evaluators. The responses are findings. But those who responded engaged in process use in that, by reading the survey's definition of process use and answering the question about it, they were learning about the concept, reflecting on it and perhaps deepening their understanding of it, thereby perhaps increasing the likelihood that they would attend to it in their practice.

Findings Use

While we are exploring process use, let us look at the concept's partner, *findings use.* Despite some thirty-five years of research on and gnashing of teeth about findings use, we have no agreed-on operational definition. We have nominal definitions of types (instrumental, enlightenment, persuasive) but no generally accepted operational definition or measuring instrument for findings use. My own utilization-focused definition of instrumental use—*intended use by intended users*—is inherently situational and context-dependent (the essence of a sensitizing concept). Indeed, rather than becoming more specific and operational in our approach to findings use, we are becoming vaguer and more general, as evidenced by the recent attention to evaluation "influence" in lieu of use (Kirkhart, 2000; Mark, 2006).

I embrace, then, the vagueness and abstractness of process use as a sensitizing concept. The concept can perhaps fulfill the function of being a usefulism, without its merit and worth being judged by the extent to which it can be precisely operationalized. This means it has to be defined situationally, that its meaning is context-dependent, and that its utility is to encourage dialogue about the many and diverse uses of evaluation.

Deepening Our Understanding of Process Use

The chapters and case examples in this volume present in-depth examples of process use, deepen our understanding of how it can be manifested, explore its implications for evaluation practice, and raise further issues for clarification and dialogue. Let me highlight some of the issues raised.

Evaluation Capacity Building (ECB), Intentionality, and Process Use. All of the chapters in this volume deal in some way with the relationship between building evaluation capacity and process use (p. 8). Harnar and Preskill believe that process use reflects "incidental learning" and is a "by-product" of stakeholders' engagement, while "ECB [evaluation capacity building] represents the evaluator's clear intentions to build learning into the evaluation process" (p. 40). King, in contrast (Chapter Three), sees intentional process use as having the practical effect of building the evaluation capacity of an organization and suggests that "process use and ECB may well be a marriage made in heaven" (p. 46). King also comments that, "Without knowing it, for almost thirty years I have engaged in and fostered process use during program evaluations in a range of educational and social service settings" (p. 45). She values the increased intentionality that identifying, recognizing, and labeling process use enables, and she now engages intentionally in facilitating process use; but her experience makes clear that process use as an outcome of evaluation participation can occur through varying degrees of intentionality. Table 1.1 in the Amo and Cousins chapter makes ECB part of "evaluative inquiry" while process use (and findings use) are "evaluation consequences"; in their model, both ECB and process use contribute to evaluation capacity and organizational learning capacity. Carden and Earl aim to make evaluation a useful process that develops the evaluation capacity of everyone involved, thereby nurturing "the deep culture of evaluation and evaluative thinking the Evaluation Unit has built at IDRC" (p. 61). Lawrenz, Huffman, and McGinnis, in their case study of a multisite evaluation effort (Chapter Five), found that use of evaluation processes was related to site-based variations in evaluation capacity; sites with more capacity engaged in a wider range of evaluation tasks. Podems' South Africa case (Chapter Six) examines how process use can emerge in a situation where programs have no initial evaluation capacity or understanding.

So, let us see what we can sort out about the relationship between process use and ECB. First, Harnar and Preskill seem to confuse the activity (ECB) with the outcome (process use). This is like confusing methods of data collection with findings. The Amo and Cousins conceptualization maintains this distinction between the activity (ECB) and the outcome (process use). Process use is not itself capacity building; rather, it is capacity *built* (see Table 1.1 in Chapter One). If an evaluation includes explicit ECB, and if that ECB is effective, then evaluation capacity is built, meaning that a *result* of the evaluation process is process use (capacity built).

King's chapter, in this vein, refers to embedding evaluative thinking in an organization as "the ultimate goal, the dependent variable, of my evaluation practice" (p. 47). This is the outcome of ECB. When she discusses "how to make process use an independent variable in evaluation practice: the purposeful means of building an organization's capacity to conduct and use evaluations in the long run" (p. 45), I think she is distinguishing process use as a short-term outcome from the cumulative long-term impact of evaluative thinking embedded in the organization's culture, as depicted in Figure 7.1. The long-term, cumulative impact is by no means certain or inevitable, as King illustrates in sharing her extensive experiences and insights.

While we are on the topic of diagrams, my main suggestion about the comprehensive Amo and Cousins model is that a feedback arrow could be added from evaluation consequences directly back to evaluation inquiry because both process use and findings use (especially in combination) can affect evaluation inquiry. This can occur both within the life of a particular evaluation (because process use and findings use can happen *during* an evaluation) and in subsequent or parallel evaluation inquiries (those going on at the same time). The feedback relationship would add a more dynamic systems dimension to their framework (see Figure 7.2).

Figure 7.1. Longitudinal Perspective on ECB Leading to Cumulative Process Use

Figure 7.2. Interactive Relationship Between Evaluation Inquiry and Evaluation Consequences

Second, degree of intentionality cuts across findings use and process use, a point emphasized in Kirkhart's "Integrated Theory of Influence" (2000) and illustrated in Table 7.1.

Intended process use can include ECB, but *not all intended process use involves ECB*. Intentionally using the evaluation process to deepen shared program understandings or reinforce the program intervention is intended process use that has nothing to do with ECB. Indeed, much process use has a greater and more direct impact on program or organization processes and effectiveness than on evaluative capacity itself. So, contrary to the Harnar and Preskill proposal, I do not find it conceptually clarifying to consider process use an incidental by-product while ECB is viewed as distinctly intentional, especially given the "gray area" in Table 7.1.

Third, not all ECB involves process use. Process use refers to impacts that flow from being engaged in and experiencing some actual evaluation process. Much ECB is freestanding and not part of an evaluation process. For example, direct training of program staff and evaluators is a form of ECB. ECB is process use only when such training (or other ECB activity) is part of a larger evaluation experience. Moreover, as King's chapter emphasizes, ECB involves a continuum of engagement with evaluation from none to full integration (evaluative inquiry as a way of life, her "free-range evaluation").

Fourth, not all ECB is intentional. Most stakeholders participating in an evaluation are doing so to get a specific evaluation conducted and attain findings, not to enhance their organization's evaluation capacity. Much ECB, then, is implicit and unintended *from the perspective of those involved* even if intended (or at least hoped for) by the evaluation facilitator. This distinction is critical; this is the gray area of process use shown in Table 7.1. I may

Table 7.1. Matrix of Intentionality and Use/Influence

	Findings Use and Influence	Process Uses and Influences
Intended	Intended use by intended users	Includes explicit, planned ECB, as well as other process uses
Intended or unintended; gray area	Intentionality focused on primary intended users, but planned dissemination *hopes for* broader influence (though can't be sure if or where this will occur)	Evaluator facilitates the evaluation process to build capacity, but this is implicit and those stakeholders who are involved are motivated by, and focused on, findings use
Unintended	Unplanned influence of findings beyond primary intended users—and even beyond original dissemination	ECB implicit (an artifact of participation in the evaluation)

facilitate an evaluation focusing on intended findings use but also intending, by the way I facilitate, to engender some process use; from the perspective of those involved, the intentionality is about findings use, and they become aware of process use only in reflecting after the experience. King also notes how unintentional ECB can occur: "people may inadvertently learn evaluation skills" (p. 46) from an evaluator conducting an evaluation with no intentional ECB goals. I would add to this the case where a stakeholder participates in an evaluation to intentionally learn evaluation skills even though this is not the intention of the evaluator, who is focused only on findings use.

Ethical Challenges. Anyone in close proximity to an evaluation can benefit from—be a user of—the process. The Podems chapter shows not only how program staff (in her case, agency directors) learn from and change behaviors as the result of an evaluation, but also the ethical dilemmas that can emerge about how far to push process use. When an evaluator knows things about a funder's perspective that would benefit a program, how this information is handled has both ethical dimensions and process-use implications. Because an evaluator often negotiates the design with the funder, it can be quite common for the evaluator to learn things that program directors do not know—and realize that fact only during fieldwork. Thus the Podems chapter highlights the difficult and ambiguous ethical issues that can accompany attention to process use. I would recommend using the Podems chapter as a teaching case with students to stimulate dialogue about real-world ethical challenges.

Users of Process Use. The original focus of process use (Patton, 1997, 1998) was on program stakeholders who participate in an evaluation. The multisite evaluation case in Chapter Five illustrates that evaluators can also be affected by, and users of, evaluation processes for learning. As the local evaluators conducted evaluations under the multisite design, the skills and knowledge of those local evaluators were subject to process use.

The Dark Side

As I write this, the media are celebrating the thirtieth anniversary of the first *Star Wars* film, which makes Star Wars and evaluation generational siblings. *Star Wars,* like evaluation, is about distinguishing good from bad. The examples of process use in this volume illustrate positive examples—the "good." But just as attention to findings use now includes concern about misuse, it seems appropriate to inquire into the dark side of process use. What are examples of misusing evaluation processes?

Going through an evaluation *to justify a decision already made* (that is, giving the false impression that the evaluation findings will be used) abuses the evaluation process, in that it wastes scarce evaluation resources and contributes to organizational skepticism about evaluation. This is the shadow side of evaluation contributing to a program culture of learning or embedding evaluative thinking in the organization. Instead, false and inauthentic evaluation processes foster staff skepticism about, and resistance to, future evaluation efforts. I hear allegations that the U.S. government's Program Assessment Rating Tool (PART) falls in this category, in that it is a highly politicized and compliance-oriented process administered to give the appearance that there is accountability and an empirical basis for decisions that, in reality, are made on purely political criteria.

Imposing randomized, controlled trial (RCT) designs because they are held up as the gold standard can constitute evaluation process abuse, in my view, because methods decisions are distorted. The most basic wisdom in evaluation is that you begin by assessing the situation, figure out what information is needed, determine the relevant questions, and then select methods to answer those questions. However, when RCTs are treated as the gold standard, evaluators and funders *begin* by asking: "How can we do an RCT?" This puts the method *before* the question. It also creates perverse incentives. For example, in some agencies, project managers are getting positive performance reviews and even bonuses for supporting and conducting RCTs. Under such incentives, project managers will seek to do RCTs whether they are appropriate or not. No one wants to do a second-rate evaluation; but if RCTs are really the gold standard, then anything else is second-rate.

This also leads to imposing RCT designs before the program is ready for such summative evaluation. For example, an influential report from the Center for Global Development advocates RCTs for impact evaluation of international development aid, arguing that such trials "must be considered from the start—the design phase—rather than after the program has been operating for many years." (Evaluation Gap Working Group, 2006, p. 13). At first blush, this sounds reasonable, but for an RCT to work, an intervention (program) must be stabilized and standardized. This means you would not evaluate a new initiative with an RCT before doing formative evaluation to work out bugs, overcome initial implementation problems, and stabilize the intervention. Not even drug studies begin with RCTs. They begin with basic efficacy and dosage studies to find out if there is preliminary evidence that the drug produces the desired outcome without unacceptable side effects. Only then are RCTs undertaken. Imposing RCTs on new programs without a formative period amounts to using the evaluation design to rigidly control and interfere with program adaptability— a potential misuse of evaluation. The Joint Committee (1994) feasibility standard on "practical procedures" states: "The evaluation procedures should be practical, to keep disruption to a minimum while needed information is obtained" (F1). By this standard, evaluation designs that interfere with effective program implementation would constitute evaluation process misuse.

Table 7.2 presents examples of positive and negative process uses (acknowledging that one person's positive use may be another's abuse, and vice versa).

Table 7.2. Process Use: Positive Outcomes and Potential Misuses

Type of Process Use	Positive Outcomes	Potential Process Misuses (or Perceived Abuses)
1. Infusing evaluative thinking into organizational culture	Evaluation becomes part of the organization's way of doing business, contributing to all aspects of organizational effectiveness; people speak the same language, share meanings and priorities; reduces resistance to evaluation	Lots of rhetoric from leadership about valuing evaluative thinking, but the rhetoric is used to provide cover for highly politicized decision making; the false rhetoric actually deepens skepticism about evaluation and increases resistance
2. Enhancing shared understandings within the program	Gets everyone on the same page; supports alignment of resources with program priorities	Those with more power use evaluation to impose their own preferred criteria or perspective on those with less power
3. Supporting and reinforcing the program intervention	Enhances outcomes and increases program impacts; increases the value (cost-benefit) of the evaluation; the evaluation is integrated into the program, as when evaluative reflection is part of the program experience	Distorts the independent purpose of evaluation; the effects of the program become intertwined with the effects of the evaluation, making the evaluation part of the intervention; leads to design, role, and purpose confusion
4. Instrumentation effects	What gets measured gets done; focuses program resources on priorities; measurement contributes to participants' learning; encourages reflection	Measure the wrong things, and the wrong things get done; what can be measured determines what the program's goals are (goal displacement); corruption of indicators, especially where the stakes become high
5. Increasing participant engagement, self-determination, and sense of ownership (empowerment)	Makes evaluation especially meaningful and understandable to participants; empowering; participants learn evaluation skills and critical thinking	Can be used to manipulate participants; done inauthentically, evaluation involvement leads to unfulfilled promises, creating alienation; disempowering
6. Program and organizational development; developmental evaluation	Builds evaluative capacity; increases adaptability; nurtures becoming a learning organization; increases overall effectiveness in program management and use of feedback	Evaluator plays nonevaluation roles and functions, which confuses the evaluation purpose, reduces the evaluator's credibility, and misinforms participants about what evaluation's primary function is (judging merit and worth, not development)

Source: Adapted from Patton (in press).

Wisdom and Process Use

In 1950, the renowned psychoanalyst Erik Erikson conceptualized the phases of life, identifying wisdom as a likely (but not inevitable) by-product of aging; it is a finding I myself strangely resonate with. Wisdom becomes ascendant during the eighth and final stage of psychosocial development, a time of "ego integrity versus despair." Ego integrity counters the potential despair of increasing infirmity and approaching death, yielding mellowness-inducing wisdom. Erikson, however, never operationalized wisdom, and a half-century later, psychologists still do not agree on what it is or how to measure it (Hall, 2007).

I experience wisdom as a usefulism—a sensitizing concept, something to ponder, look for, and dialogue about. I confess that the possibility of at least one positive outcome of aging gives me some comfort, as does the possibility that all the hard work of facilitating an evaluation process may yield more enduring outcomes for participants than only findings (as important as they may be), for their relevance diminishes rapidly. Who knows? Perhaps helping people learn to *think evaluatively* will nurture ego integrity, fend off despair (that nothing works), and lead to wisdom. Add wisdom to the list of process use outcomes.

References

Blumer, H. "What Is Wrong with Social Theory?" *American Sociological Review,* 1954, 19, 3–10.

Cousins, J. B., and Shulha, L. M. "A Comparative Analysis of Evaluation Utilization and Its Cognate Fields of Inquiry: Current Issues and Trends." In I. Shaw, J. Greene, and M. Mark (eds.), *The Sage Handbook of Evaluation: Policies, Programs and Practices.* Thousand Oaks, Calif.: Sage, 2006.

Evaluation Gap Working Group. *When Will We Ever Learn? Improving Lives Through Impact Evaluation.* Washington, D.C.: Center for Global Development, 2006 (http://www.cgdev.org/section/initiatives/_active/evalgap).

Hall, S. S. "The Older-and-Wiser Hypothesis." *Sunday New York Times Magazine,* May 6, 2007 (http://www.nytimes.com/ref/magazine/20070430_WISDOM.html).

Joint Committee on Standards for Educational Evaluation. *The Program Evaluation Standards.* Thousand Oaks, Calif.: Sage, 1994.

Kirkhart, K. E. "Reconceptualizing Evaluation Use: An Integrated Theory of Influence." In V. Caracelli and H. Preskill (eds.), *The Expanding Scope of Evaluation Use. New Directions for Evaluation,* no. 88. San Francisco: Jossey-Bass, 2000.

Mark, M. "The Consequences of Evaluation: Theory, Research, and Practice." Plenary Presidential Address, Annual Conference of the American Evaluation Association, Nov. 2, 2006, Portland, Ore.

Mueller, C. W. "Conceptualization, Operationalization, and Measurement." In M. S. Lewis-Beck, A. Bryman, and T. Futing Liao (eds.), *The Sage Encyclopedia of Social Science Research Methods.* Thousand Oaks, Calif.: Sage, 2004.

Patton, M. Q. *Utilization-Focused Evaluation* (3rd ed.). Thousand Oaks, Calif.: Sage, 1997.

Patton, M. Q. "Discovering Process Use." *Evaluation,* 1998, 4(2), 225–233.

Patton, M. *Utilization-Focused Evaluation* (4th. ed.). Thousand Oaks, Calif.: Sage, in press.

Safire, W. "Halfway Humanity." (On Language.) *Sunday New York Times Magazine,* May 6, 2007 (http://www.nytimes.com/2007/05/06/magazine/06wwln-safire-t.html).

Schwandt, T. *Dictionary of Qualitative Inquiry* (2nd rev. ed.). Thousand Oaks, Calif.: Sage, 2001.

Wiebeck, V., and Dahlgren, M. "Learning in Focus Groups: An Analytical Dimension for Enhancing Focus Group Research." *Qualitative Research*, 2007, 7(2), 249–267.

Williams, M. "Operationism/Operationalism." In M. S. Lewis-Beck, A. Bryman, and T. Futing Liao (eds.), *The Sage Encyclopedia of Social Science Research Methods*. Thousand Oaks, Calif.: Sage, 2004.

MICHAEL QUINN PATTON is an independent organizational development and evaluation consultant.

INDEX

NEW DIRECTIONS FOR EVALUATION
Order Form
SUBSCRIPTIONS AND SINGLE ISSUES

DISCOUNTED BACK ISSUES:

Use this form to receive **20% off** all back issues of New Directions for Evaluation. All single issues priced at **$21.60** (normally $29.00)

TITLE	ISSUE NO.	ISBN

Call 888-378-2537 or see mailing instructions below. When calling, mention the promotional code, JB7ND, to receive your discount.

SUBSCRIPTIONS: (1 year, 4 issues)

☐ New Order   ☐ Renewal

U.S.	☐ Individual: $85	☐ Institutional: $215
Canada/Mexico	☐ Individual: $85	☐ Institutional: $255
All Others	☐ Individual: $109	☐ Institutional: $289

Call 888-378-2537 or see mailing and pricing instructions below. Online subscriptions are available at www.interscience.wiley.com.

Copy or detach page and send to:
**John Wiley & Sons, Journals Dept, 5th Floor
989 Market Street, San Francisco, CA 94103-1741**
Order Form can also be faxed to: 888-481-2665

Issue/Subscription Amount: $ _____

Shipping Amount: $ _____
(for single issues only—subscription prices include shipping)

Total Amount: $ _____

SHIPPING CHARGES:		
SURFACE	Domestic	Canadian
First Item	$5.00	$6.00
Each Add'l Item	$3.00	$1.50

(No sales tax for U.S. subscriptions. Canadian residents, add GST for subscription orders. Individual rate subscriptions must be paid by personal check or credit card. Individual rate subscriptions may not be resold as library copies.)

☐ Payment enclosed (U.S. check or money order only. All payments must be in U.S. dollars.)

☐ VISA ☐ MC ☐ Amex # _____ Exp. Date _____

Card Holder Name _____ Card Issue # _____

Signature_____ Day Phone _____

☐ Bill Me (U.S. institutional orders only. Purchase order required.)

Purchase order # _____

Federal Tax ID13559302   GST 89102 8052

Name _____

Address _____

Phone _____ E-mail _____

JB7ND

NEW DIRECTIONS FOR EVALUATION
IS NOW AVAILABLE ONLINE AT WILEY INTERSCIENCE

What is Wiley InterScience?

Wiley InterScience is the dynamic online content service from John Wiley & Sons delivering the full text of over 300 leading scientific, technical, medical, and professional journals, plus major reference works, the acclaimed Current Protocols laboratory manuals, and even the full text of select Wiley print books online.

What are some special features of Wiley InterScience?

Wiley Interscience Alerts is a service that delivers table of contents via e-mail for any journal available on Wiley InterScience as soon as a new issue is published online.
Early View is Wiley's exclusive service presenting individual articles online as soon as they are ready, even before the release of the compiled print issue. These articles are complete, peer-reviewed, and citable.
CrossRef is the innovative multi-publisher reference linking system enabling readers to move seamlessly from a reference in a journal article to the cited publication, typically located on a different server and published by a different publisher.

How can I access Wiley InterScience?

Visit http://www.interscience.wiley.com.

Guest Users can browse Wiley InterScience for unrestricted access to journal Tables of Contents and Article Abstracts, or use the powerful search engine.
Registered Users are provided with a *Personal Home Page* to store and manage customized alerts, searches, and links to favorite journals and articles. Additionally, Registered Users can view free Online Sample Issues and preview selected material from major reference works.
Licensed Customers are entitled to access full-text journal articles in PDF, with select journals also offering full-text HTML.

How do I become an Authorized User?

Authorized Users are individuals authorized by a paying Customer to have access to the journals in Wiley InterScience. For example, a University that subscribes to Wiley journals is considered to be the Customer. Faculty, staff and students authorized by the University to have access to those journals in Wiley InterScience are Authorized Users. Users should contact their Library for information on which Wiley journals they have access to in Wiley InterScience.

ASK YOUR INSTITUTION ABOUT WILEY INTERSCIENCE TODAY!

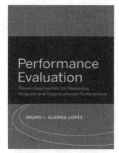

Performance Evaluation
Proven Approaches for Improving Program and Organizational Performance

Ingrid J. Guerra-Lopez
Paperback, 250 pages
ISBN 978-0-7879-8883-8

Using this resource, readers will be able to implement the most appropriate scientifically based evaluations model in a variety of situations. It offers a guide for practitioners, researchers, and educators for the understanding and application of scientifically based evaluations that are both rigorous and flexible. The book covers seven major evaluation models and the author, a highly experienced academic and consultant evaluator, bridges the gap between theory and practice by illustrating the various approaches in simple language. The book explores the research evidence behind the utility of each model, shows how each approach looks in practice, and explains why it works for one situation and not another. Academically, the author is rooted in both education and public administration, areas that often share evaluation and needs assessment courses.

Ingrid J Guerra-Lopez is an associate research professor at the Sonora Institute of Technology in Mexico and consults for public and private organizations, specifically in the areas of performance measurement and tracking.

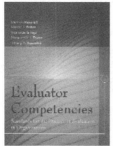

Evaluator Competencies
Standards for the Practice of Evaluation in Organizations

Darlene F. Russ-Eft, Marcie J. Bober, Ileana de la Teja,
Marguerite Foxon, Tiffany A. Koszalka
Hardcover, 200 pages
ISBN 978-0-7879-9599-7

This guide to evaluator competencies will enhance the effectiveness of evaluators in training and in practice. Written by a team of experts in the area of evaluation and sponsored by the leading organization for performance standards (International Board of Standards for Training, Performance, and Instruction), *Evaluator Competencies* presents validated evaluator competencies with practical and applicable description of each of these competencies. The book discusses the challenges and obstacles in conducting such evaluations within dynamic, changing organizations, and provides methods and strategies for putting these competencies to use. The book also identifies alternative approaches to overcoming these challenges and obstacles.

Darlene Russ-Eft, Ph.D., is Associate Professor within the Department of Adult Education and Higher Education Leadership within the College of Education at Oregon State University. Her teaching focuses on program evaluation, research methods, and learning theory.

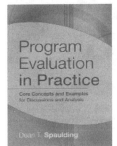

Program Evaluation in Practice
Core Concepts and Examples for Discussion and Analysis

Dean T. Spaulding
Paperback, 368 pages
ISBN 978-0-7879-8685-8

This ground-breaking book of teaching cases covers the essentials of program evaluation. A wide variety of evaluation projects are discussed, analyzed, and reflected upon. The book covers the essentials of program evaluation, including foundation and types of evaluation, tools for collecting data, writing reports, and sharing findings. Individual cases cover classroom instruction, community-based program, teacher training, professional development, a secondary-school based program, after-school program, reading achievement, school-improvement grant, and confidentiality.

Each case includes learning objectives, program description, evaluation plan, summary of evaluation activities and findings, key concepts, discussion questions, class activities, and suggested reading. As useful for students as it is for evaluators in training, it is a must-have for those aspiring to become effective evaluators.

Dean T. Spaulding teaches at the College of Saint Rose in Albany, New York. He is the chair of the Teaching Evaluation SIG for the American Evaluation Association.

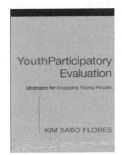

Youth Participatory Evaluation
Strategies for Engaging Young People

Kim Sabo Flores
Paperback, 208 pages
ISBN 978-0-7879-8392-5

This groundbreaking book explores why youth participatory evaluation (YPE) has become so important so quickly. A "how to" guide to participatory research and evaluation, it provides step-by-step, playful, and accessible activities that have proven effective and can be used by evaluators, educators, youth workers, researchers, funders, and children's and human rights advocates in their efforts to more effectively engage young people.

Positioning program evaluation as a fundamental piece of the participatory research field, it includes everything from history to theory to core concepts to practical tips—a complete approach to effective participatory research and evaluation with youth. It also offers substantial theory and experience to provide a fundamental component of professional preparation and leading-edge practice.

Kim Sabo is the founder of Kim Sabo Consulting, a research and evaluation organization that focuses on participatory planning and evaluation for nonprofit organizations. She previously served on the faculty of the Graduate School of the City University of New York.

Mixed Methods in Social Inquiry

Jennifer C. Greene
Paperback, 232 pages
ISBN: 978-0-7879-8382-6

"An excellent addition to the literature of integrated methodology . . . The author has skillfully integrated diverse ways of thinking about mixed methods into a comprehensive and meaningful framework. She makes it easy for both the students and the practitioners to understand the intricate details and complexities of doing mixed methods research."
—ABBAS TASHAKKORI, Frost Professor and coordinator, educational research and evaluation methodology, Department of Educational and Psychological Studies, Florida International University, founding coeditor, *Journal of Mixed Methods Research*

"This is the best available book on the topic for both scholars and students."
—MARY LEE SMITH, regents professor, Arizona State University

Jennifer Greene is professor in quantitative and evaluative research methodologies, Department of Educational Psychology, College of Education, at the University of Illinois, Champaign.

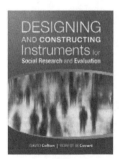

Designing and Constructing Instruments for Social Research and Evaluation

David Colton, Robert W. Covert
Paperback, 412 pages
ISBN: 978-0-7879-8784-8

A comprehensive step-by-step guide to creating effective surveys, polls, questionnaires, customer satisfaction forms, ratings, checklists, and other instruments. This book can be used by those who are developing instruments for the first time and those who want to hone their skills.

This book provides a thorough presentation of instrument construction, from conception to development and pretesting of items, formatting the instrument, administration, and, finally, data management and presentation of the findings. Included are guidelines for reviewing and revising the questionnaire to enhance validity and reliability, and for working effectively with stakeholders such as instrument designers, decision-makers, agency personnel, clients, and raters or respondents.

David Colton, Ph.D., is adjunct professor and Robert W. Covert, Ph.D., is associate professor at the University of Virginia's Curry School of Graduate Studies in the program in Research, Statistics, and Evaluation.

Research Methods and Evaluation Books of Interest

The Telephone Interviewer's Handbook
How to Conduct Standardized Conversations

Patricia A. Gwartney
Paperback, 336 pages
ISBN 978-0-7879-8638-4

This essential resource offers training on all aspects of conducting telephone interviews. It reviews the types of surveys, the interviewer's role in the survey process, survey research, ethics, laws that protect telephone interviewing, and respondents' rights. It also details the job of interviewing, including respondent selection procedures and addressing respondents' concerns about a wide range of situations. The book highlights how to record dial attempts, how to input respondents' answers, how to move from screen to screen, and how to read and evaluate call histories. It offers universal guidelines, such as common problems implementing the call disposition codes recommended by major professional associations. The author discusses interviewers' responsibilities, explaining their key role in the survey process, and how to motivate them to do their best. A special section addresses the persons who hire, train, monitor, coordinate, and supervise telephone interviewers.

Patricia A. Gwartney, Ph.D., is Professor of Sociology at the University of Oregon, Eugene. An internationally known expert in the field of survey research, she was the Founding Director of the University of Oregon Survey Research Laboratory (OSRL).

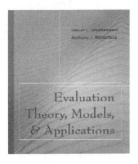

Evaluation Theory, Models & Applications

Daniel L. Stufflebeam, Anthony J. Shinkfield
Hardcover, 768 pages
ISBN: 978-0-7879-7765-8

This comprehensive resource helps you develop a commanding knowledge of the evaluation field: its history, theory, standards, models, approaches, and procedures. You'll learn to identify, analyze, and judge 26 evaluation approaches and apply standards to discriminate among legitimate and illicit approaches.

A textbook and a handbook, it includes down-to-earth procedures, checklists, and illustrations of how to carry out a sequence of essential evaluation tasks; identify and assess evaluation opportunities; prepare an institution to support a projected evaluation; design, budget, and contract evaluations; collect, analyze, and synthesize information; and report and facilitate use of findings.

Daniel L. Stufflebeam, Ph.D., is Distinguished University Professor and Harold and Beulah McKee Professor of Education at Western Michigan University, Kalamazoo.

Anthony J. Shinkfield, Ed.D., has served in numerous positions in education leadership, including assistant director, Research and Planning Directorate, Education Department of South Australia.